Earn College Credit for What You Know

Fourth Edition

Janet Colvin

CAEL

The Council for Adult & Experiential Learning
Chicago

KENDALL/HUNT PUBLISHING COMPANY
4050 Westmark Drive Dubuque, Iowa 52002

 CAEL

The Council for Adult & Experiential Learning
55 East Monroe Street, Suite 1930
Chicago, Illinois 60603

© 1992, 1996, 1997, 2006 The Council for Adult & Experiential Learning
(CAEL)

ISBN 0-7575-2750-7

Manufactured in the United States of America
10 9 8 7 6 5 4 3 2 1

To John

Contents

Acknowledgements

- I salute Susan Simosko and Lois Lamdin who authored previous editions of the book.
- I acknowledge and give thanks for the leadership of Pamela Tate and Morris Keeton the current and past CEO's of the Council for Adult and Experiential Learning (CAEL).
- I thank PLA practitioners and leaders who have influenced me including Patricia Dewees, Donna Younger, Kaye Woodward, Theresa Hoffman, Victoria Ferrara, Ruth Frey, and the dedicated staff and consultants at CAEL. Thanks to practitioners for input on my blog: http://platalk.typepad.com/.
- Thanks to my colleagues from Regis University including Margo Rosencrantz, Sharon Leonard, Fran Kehoe, Bea Jennings, Cyndy Redifer, Kristi Frush, Elise Sweet, Mary Martin, Mike Zizzi, Larry Seid, and Becky Smith-Eggeman.
- My applause to researchers and authors in the field of prior learning assessment including Urban Whitaker, Tom Flint, Barry Sheckley, Elana Michelson and Alan Mandell.
- I appreciate the students at Regis University who have inspired me with their thirst for learning. It has been an honor to guide you in the portfolio process during the last 14 years.
- I tip my hat to students across the country who talked with me about their experience with portfolio assessment including Andrew Robinson, Jay Brewer, Ty Rhyne, Antelia Salazar-Ball, Maria Gonzales, Tim Lee, George Dow, and Rachel Baxter.
- More appreciation to Susan Kannel for the privilege of serving as the "contact us" person on CAEL's NACTEL and EPCE partnership web sites (www.nactel.org; www.epceonline.org).
- I am grateful to Carolyn Mann and Bonnie Cline for their reviews and to Heidi Moore for her editing.
- Kudos to Bernadette Dubs for editing the final proofs.

- I am indebted to Diana Bamford-Rees' leadership that brought this book to completion.

In closing, I've had the privilege of a supportive family, group of friends, and a big God.

I believe the growth in prior learning assessment programs in higher education will inspire more students to earn college credit for what they know.

Janet Colvin
Denver, Colorado
December 5, 2005

Note on the Format

Since I answer a large volume of inquiries from students on prior learning assessment from CAEL partnership Web sites, I decided to use a FAQ-style question and answer format for the book. I believe that most busy adults appreciate reading answers to the most commonly-asked questions about prior learning assessment.

This book does not take a cookie-cutter approach to portfolio assessment. I recognize that every program and institution has different standards. The methods represented are not intended to prescribe the best approach or best practices.

The excerpt in the Appendix from "Maria" is fictional but is based on actual students' experiences. The names of people and companies have been changed to respect identities.

Introduction

In our current economy, it is more important than ever before to obtain a college degree. According to the Bureau of Labor Statistics (2004–05), jobs requiring an associate's degree are projected to grow by 31 percent, accounting for more than one million jobs by 2008. Additionally, jobs requiring at least a bachelor's degree will account for about 12.7 million job openings through 2008. *Earn College Credit for What You Know* is written for the millions of adults who have acquired learning outside traditional college classrooms and provides valuable guidance for exploring options for obtaining college credits to meet the degree requirements that the current job market demands.

CAEL first published *Earn College Credit for What You Know* in 1985 with second and third editions following in 1992 and 1996. In the 20 years since the publication of the first edition, higher education and adult learning have changed dramatically. Adult learning continues to grow in importance in this country as well as around the world. Adult learners represent a large, and growing, proportion of higher education enrollments and the "nontraditional" adult student has become the norm in many institutions. This fourth edition of *Earn College Credit for What You Know* acknowledges this new majority's impact on higher education and the workplace, and incorporates new information about Prior Learning Assessment (PLA) practices and policies. It also recognizes the important role online learning and online assessment play for adult learners, as online delivery has become the fastest growing channel through which adults learn while maintaining a full-time work and family schedule.

Earn College Credit for What You Know is written in accord with CAEL's ten standards of good practice in the assessment of learning for credit (see Chapter 4) and is dedicated to helping you receive recognition for what you have learned. The assessment methods described in this book represent valid methods of earning academic credit for knowledge acquired in a variety of settings outside of the classroom, e.g., company sponsored training programs, volunteer activities, union activities, hobbies, etc. The CAEL standards for assessing learning are reviewed and expanded periodically to reflect recent innovations in the field. Please visit the CAEL website at www.cael.org for the most current version of these assessment standards.

We have divided the book into four sections. Part I addresses the *process* of Prior Learning Assessment (PLA), and provides an introduction to prior learning assessment, samples of adult learner profiles, information on educational goal-setting and prior learning assessment planning, and introduces the CAEL standards for assessment. Part II provides information on ways to obtain credit for transcripts and corporate training and describes options for credit by examination. Part III reviews learning theory and the "how to" of developing a portfolio for learning assessment. The fourth part of the book, a substantive appendix, contains guidance for finding institutions that offer PLA, instructions on creating a prior learning inventory, and samples of components of a prior learning portfolio.

We know you will find this book helpful, and we wish you much success as you strive to gain the credit you deserve!

Diana Bamford-Rees
Associate Vice President
CAEL
January 2006

PART

I

The
Prior Learning
Assessment Process

CHAPTER 1

Introduction to Prior Learning Assessment

Thousands of adult learners have successfully used a variety of assessment methods to earn college credit for what they know. Consider these students' experiences:

- Andrew thought he would feel out of place when he returned to college as an adult. He had quit college when he was younger in order to provide income for his family. Twenty years later, Andrew enrolled in a program that was tailored to working adults, and he found the college atmosphere exhilarating. After learning about the portfolio method of earning college credit for his prior learning, Andrew earned a total of 39 credit hours in such areas as psychology, video production, and public speaking. The portfolio method provided momentum for Andrew to pursue his educational goals. After finishing his bachelor's degree, Andrew completed his master's degree and is currently pursuing a doctorate.

- After receiving tuition benefits through his workplace, Tim was ready to earn his bachelor's degree, the piece of paper that kept him from achieving the same success as his colleagues at a software development company. After several years of starting and quitting college, Tim was determined to finish. He received 14 credits for military training, passed a College Level Examination Program (CLEP) exam for a total of six credits, and passed an in-house college challenge exam in UNIX. Tim earned 22 credits through the portfolio method for his broad experiences in Web development, process mapping, business communication, and project management. He benefited from American Council on Education's (ACE) College Credit Recommendation Service to earn credit for a computer certification. These methods earned Tim a total of 32 college credits—the equivalent of more than a full year of credits toward his bachelor's degree.

- Maria thought her years working out of her home as a licensed day care provider while she was a stay-at-home mom and as an educator in two nonprofit settings wouldn't hold much value toward the associate degree she desired. However, after consulting with an academic advisor and petitioning for credit through the portfolio method, she earned a total of 11 credits for her learning in first aid, early childhood education methods, comparing cultures, communication, and introductory piano. Maria applied six credits toward her degree by passing a Spanish CLEP exam; this quickly moved her 17 credits closer to completion of her associate degree.

The experiences of these adult students, who represent just a few of the millions worldwide, reinforce the notion that learning outside the college classroom is valuable, lifelong, and, in some cases, useful for earning college credit. In fact, according to the Lumina Foundation, "only one in six students fits the mold of the 'typical' 18-year-old who enrolls at a residential campus, stays four years and graduates with a baccalaureate degree. Adult students (25 years of age and older) are becoming the new majority" (2005). The testimonies in this book demonstrate how adults who have returned to college have used their rich storehouses of learning experiences to earn college credit toward their degree.

This book is intended to help adult students prepare to earn college credit for their lifelong learning. The assessment methods described in this book represent valid, yet often underused, methods of earning credit. Until more students take advantage of prior learning assessment methods, millions of potential credit hours may remain unclaimed.

College Costs

Obtaining a college degree is beneficial in an unstable job market. Many of the jobs of today didn't exist seven years ago, and it follows that today's knowledge will become outdated; in addition, outsourcing has affected manufacturing, technical, and even medical professionals. According to Morton Bahr, president of the Communications Workers of America, "Training and education will become even more important for workers, especially in tough economic times. Skills and knowledge give people career mobility so that they aren't just left on the scrap heap when a company goes under or announces a layoff" (2002, paragraph 17). Consider:

- Jobs requiring an associate degree are projected to grow by 31 percent and to add more than one million jobs by 2008 (Bureau of Labor Statistics, U.S. Department of Labor 2004–05).

- Jobs requiring at least a bachelor's degree will account for about 12.7 million job openings through 2008 (Bureau of Labor Statistics, U.S. Department of Labor, 2004–05).
- According to the Census Bureau, over an adult's working life, high school graduates earn an average of $1.2 million, associate degree holders earn about $1.6 million, and bachelor's degree holders earn about $2.1 million (Day and Newburger, 2002).

According to *U.S. News and World Report*, "Obtaining a degree has never been more important, and the cost has never been so exorbitant. Four-year tuitions at in-state colleges have jumped a staggering 85 percent in the past decade, and at community colleges, 53 percent" (Zuckerman, 2004, p. 80).

To meet the students' need for a degree at a reduced tuition cost, colleges have developed prior learning assessment programs that use standard methods for assessing and assigning college credit for a student's lifelong learning. In fact:

- Approximately half of all U.S. higher education institutions have provisions for PLA (Prior Learning Assessment), for the individualized assessment of experience-based learning (CAEL, 1999).
- Nearly half of the adult population is now participating in formal education, and the trend is rising. More than 40 million adults, over 20 percent of the adult population, are involved in work-related learning (Voorhees & Lingenfelter, 2003).
- ACE has reviewed thousands of corporate, labor unions, government agencies, schools, and military training programs for college credit recommendations (ACE, 2005).
- About 2,900 colleges grant credit or advanced standing for CLEP exams. Nearly half of them also administer the exams at their own CLEP test centers. In many cases, students can earn up to 30 credits for testing (College Board 2005).

What Is Prior Learning Assessment?

Prior Learning Assessment (PLA) or the Assessment of Prior Learning (APL) are the terms used by colleges to describe the process of earning college credit from learning acquired through a student's work, training, volunteer experiences, and personal life. The assessment methods used work in concert with coursework to help complete a student's educational goals. The process measures the quality and level of a student's experiential learning—learning that is based on experience (Kolb, 1984, see Chapter 7 for a discussion of learning theory).

PLA is an active process that helps students determine what they know and what they need to learn through coursework. In the process, students gain confidence in their ability to work at a college level. The credits earned also puts them closer to graduation. Additionally, the active process of unpacking the learning reveals insights into areas such as writing, communication, business, and problem-solving skills.

PLA recognizes that adults bring tremendous assets to the classroom because they have more professional and personal experience, have a desire to learn, are more willing to ask questions for a deeper understanding, and typically achieve higher grades than traditional-aged college students.

PLA recognizes that learning is a lifelong activity. The average lifespan in the U.S. is now into the 80s. Since learning occurs throughout the lifespan, no student is too old to finish a college degree.

What Assessment Methods Are Commonly Used?

Assessment methods vary (see Box 1.1 below), depending on the college and subject matter.

The ideal assessment of a candidate's prior learning would require evaluators to look into their students' past; to shadow them as they applied skills, knowledge, and abilities in action; to ask questions to help synthesize their

BOX 1.1   Assessment Methods

- Credit by examination
- Development of a portfolio of prior learning with supporting documentation
- Transfer credit evaluation
- Training and certifications evaluation
- Placement exams
- Simulations
- Interviews
- Work sample evaluation
- Demonstration
- Prepared speeches
- Interviews

learning; and, finally, to determine if the learning is the equivalent of college level. Since this type of assessment would be impossible and far too time consuming for evaluators, colleges have depended on both national and local assessment strategies to determine credit. ("Colleges" is the term used in this book to describe institutions of higher education and refers to both colleges and universities.) Some assessment methods are standardized and measure general knowledge; others, such as simulations, are designed to measure a specific competency such as a medical or technical skill.

Assessment methods help reduce students' frustrations by placing them in the correct level. After all, if an advanced performer were placed in a beginning course, he or she would likely feel frustrated at the repetition of instruction on the basics. The assessment process provides very useful information for the student because it helps determine what students already know and can do and can identify gaps in their learning.

Do I Need to Be Enrolled in a College and Working Toward a Degree or Certificate to Benefit from PLA?

Generally, yes. To gain the maximum benefit for earning college credit for prior learning, students should first enroll in a two- or four-year degree or certificate program. Using assessment methods without having an educational plan is risky, especially if students want to transfer credit. On occasion, businesses, nonprofits, or government agencies use assessment methods when an employee or job candidate needs to prove college-level learning in a subject matter. Or, in rare cases, assessment methods are used for professional development. However, the majority of students who benefit from the methods described in this book are adult students enrolled in a college and working diligently toward their educational goal (see Chapters 2 and 3 on setting educational goals and plans).

What Is a Portfolio of Prior Learning?

One of the most accepted methods of earning credit involves compiling a portfolio of prior learning. A portfolio is "a formal communication, presented by the student to the college, as part of a petition requesting credit or recognition for learning outside the college classroom. The portfolio must make its case by identifying learning clearly and succinctly, and it must provide sufficient supporting information and documentation so that faculty can use it, alone or in combination with other evidence, as the basis for their evaluation" (Lamdin, 1997, p. 84). Although completing a quality portfolio is challenging, students describe this process as highly rewarding, and, in fact, many students keep and treasure their portfolio work (see Chapters 7–11 on the portfolio method).

What Subjects Are Assessed through the Portfolio Method?

Since the basis of a student's portfolio is his or her experiential learning, courses that can draw on first-hand experience, reflections, and experimentation work best. College courses or competencies weighted more heavily in theory, definitions, and concepts are better suited for testing or coursework. Many college's Web sites list the most commonly petitioned courses in their programs. Although work experience is the most frequently used context to demonstrate learning, students have received credit for volunteer and civic work, religious and spiritual pursuits, and artistic accomplishments. The list of subject areas may include (but is not limited to):

Business: introduction to business, supervision, sales, marketing, finance, project management, human resources, advertising and promotion, managing a small business, customer service, using technology for business

English and communications: technical writing, business writing, conflict resolution, public speaking, interviewing, public relations, teambuilding

Arts: photography, music, drawing, painting, art appreciation, jewelry

Computer science: computer fundamentals, database, programming, telecommunication, software competencies, Web design, networking

Social sciences: applied psychology, intercultural and ethnic studies

Education: children's literature, literacy, special education, methods

Miscellaneous: records or office management, sports/coaching, electronics

How Does the Prior Learning Portfolio Differ from Other Types of Portfolios?

The prior learning portfolio consists of written explanations that demonstrate competency targeted to a subject matter area. Also, the prior learning portfolio contains supporting documentation—such as letters, certificates, and work samples—to verify that learning. Depending on the level or subject matter being petitioned, students "leaven the mix with ample portions of reflection . . . The learning is not complete until the learner has some understanding of what both the theory and the practical experience mean" (Whitaker, 1989, p. 14). Portfolio contents are compiled in notebooks, or in some cases, saved electronically on a CD-ROM or a portfolio Web site. When completed, the portfolio is sent to an evaluator or an assessment team that determines the credit award. Commonly, portfolios are used to petition for course credit. However, some colleges grant competency credit (smaller, more specifically defined components of learning) or award multiple credits for a block of college-level learning demonstrated in the portfolio.

How Do I Know If My Learning Is College Level?

There are several determinants used to measure whether a student's learning is college level. Course outcomes (what is learned as a result of taking a course) are one measure of whether a student has achieved college-level learning. Course descriptions and course syllabi also give clues about the topics covered and level of learning required. Students who take exams can review study guides or, in some cases, take sample tests. In addition, instructors and advisors at the college are skilled in recognizing competency levels and helping students determine college-level learning. Ultimately, a trained evaluator makes the final credit decision.

How Much Credit Can I Earn?

The amount of credit a student can earn varies. Some colleges allow students to earn up to 45 credits or more through prior learning assessment. The determination on the number of credits that a student can earn is influenced by both external and internal factors. External factors include the number and level of courses that need to be fulfilled for the degree, the major and minor selected, and the institution's policies. Internal factors include the ability of the student to demonstrate her or his level of learning.

Some students accomplish a large portion of their degree plan through assessment. Students who earn large amounts of credit (21 credits or more) are frequently enrolled in a bachelor's degree program, transfer fewer credits, draw from a large storehouse of learning and documentation, and are highly motivated to complete the challenges of assessment.

One of the themes repeated throughout this book is that policies vary. There are national guidelines followed by accredited colleges for awarding credit (see Chapter 4); however, colleges have the freedom to adopt their own policies to meet the needs of their programs. Therefore, it is essential that students always check and re-check with an academic expert before proceeding with prior learning assessment.

What Are the Fees for Assessment?

Fees vary depending on the assessment methods and the college. Generally, assessment costs less than tuition—in some cases, 70 percent less than tuition fees. Some colleges add a small fee for transcription in the registrar's office (the campus location where the credit is officially recorded). The cost for credits through the portfolio method can be a one-time lump fee or a fee based on the number of credits petitioned. Some colleges offer a tuition-bearing prior learning assessment course that helps guide students through the steps of portfolio development. Because fees are subject to change, students should seek the most updated information available.

Who Is Considered a Good Candidate for PLA?

Due to the variety of college programs, it is difficult to generalize whether a student is a good candidate for credit. Below are some general characteristics of prior learning assessment candidates:

- Adult students over the age of 24 with a GED or high school diploma.
  Adult students are characterized by self-direction, work experience, and independence.

- Degree-seeking students with unfilled credit.
  The more unfilled credits students have on the degree program, the more likely the candidate will have room to plug in credits earned through prior learning assessment.

- Students who have worked under the scope of a supervisor or have worked as a supervisor or manager.
  Candidates' work experience might be as a front-line employee, customer service representative, supervisor, administrative assistant, small business owner, paraprofessional, manager, or CEO.

- Learning that can be verified.
  When using portfolio-assisted assessment, the learning must be verified by a written document such as a letter, certificate, or original artifact such as a piece of original artwork. Students are held to a higher standard of proof than a resume.

- Learning acquired that is closely matched to the outcomes or competencies required to pass a college course.

  Students are expected to have acquired the same or higher level of expertise as a student who received a passing grade in the equivalent college course.

- Learning that is applicable to a number of contexts.

  The candidate's learning should be transferable to another setting. For example, a student's skills as a supervisor and recruiter were proven to be transferable when he accepted a position with another company.

- Students whose lifelong experience is closely related to their educational goal.

  A candidate who worked as a computer programmer, for instance, could more readily apply credits toward a degree in computer science than a degree in education.

- Students who communicate with academic advisors.

  Students who are willing to listen and follow the advice of an academic advisor, mentor, prior learning specialist, or instructor are better equipped to earn credit.

Where Can I Find Institutions that Offer PLA?

Appendix 1 provides instructions on searching for colleges that offer prior learning assessment. If a candidate is using assessment methods extensively, it is important to find out the prior learning assessment policies upfront.

What Are the Benefits of PLA?

The assessment process is profitable for adult students for many reasons, including:

It gives validation.

The first benefit of earning credit for learning is that students receive validation for work and life experience. One student who gained credit through PLA stated, "I was in the workforce for 23 years before going back to college. Through assessment of prior learning, I took a hard look at what I had actually learned. It was one of the most rewarding and validating courses I have ever taken and gave me the confidence I needed to take the next step into my unknown future" (Dow, 2001, paragraph 3).

It saves time.

Earning credit for the learning gained through one's life and work may speed up the process of reaching graduation. Students are able to save time when they can focus on acquiring new knowledge and don't have to repeat what they've already learned. In addition, the flexibility helps students reach their goals and maintain their sanity while balancing school, work, and family. For students who are not ready or able to plunge into full-time coursework, the process may help them earn credit while working at a more reasonable pace. The use of technology has helped students save time because many adult-learning programs offer Web sites or online port-folio-building courses that provide e-mail access to advising services.

It saves money.

As stated, assessment saves money because the assessment fees are typi-cally less than tuition costs. In fact, a few students reported how they were able to afford to attend an institution with higher tuition costs. Prices for assessment fees vary, but compared with tuition, 30 credits earned through assessment methods could save from $600 to upward of $10,000 (if attend-ing a private college).

It helps with career and job development.

Students are finding that the portfolio-assisted assessment process is a par-ticularly beneficial process for career development. In the portfolio process, students identify the knowledge, skills, and competencies they've gained. Students have successfully used their portfolios during job interviews or performance evaluations to demonstrate competencies.

It improves critical-thinking and reflection skills.

Prior learning assessment requires that students look both backward and for-ward—backward to reflect, analyze, and sort through past learning to iden-tify gaps in learning, and forward to build on the learning (Whitaker, 1989). One study showed how the problem-solving abilities of prior learning assess-ment students were superior (compared with students lacking work experi-ence) because of their ability to reason and propose solutions based on life experiences (LeGrow, Sheckley & Kehrhahn, 2002). The ability to think criti-cally and reflect on experiences, which are skills gained in assessment, are valued highly in both academic situations and in the workplace.

What Are the Limitations of PLA?

There are often limited offerings.

This book describes the most common methods of assessment offered at colleges. Some colleges offer one or two methods; others do not assess prior learning.

The student receives a limited number of credits.

It is not possible to obtain an entire degree from experiential learning. Most colleges have a residency requirement and transfer restrictions. Obtaining a degree solely for experience is often a sales pitch used by credit mills, not accredited programs (see Box 1.2 below).

There are financial limitations.

Students should always check with a financial advisor or their company's reimbursement policy to determine if prior learning assessment fees are covered. Specifics on educational reimbursement policies are often accessible on a company's Intranet. Some government-sponsored financial aid loans do not cover fees for assessment but may cover the tuition for taking a prior learning assessment course. However, since prior learning methods are lower in cost than tuition, many students elect to pay the fees out of pocket.

There are transfer limitations.

There may be limitation on the amount of prior learning credit accepted by another college, so students who are considering transferring their credit should first check with that institution.

It is often limited to undergraduate degrees.

Prior learning assessment is often part of programs that offer undergraduate degrees for adult students, either an associate degree or bachelor's

BOX 1.2   Diploma Mills

Warning:
Beware of colleges that advertise degrees based solely on life experience. These providers defraud consumers by charging a fee and sending a fake diploma (see Chapter 5).

degree. Assessment options for graduate-level coursework (master's or doctorate degree) are less frequent.

Adults learn a tremendous amount from experience. While these learning experiences may be significant life lessons, they may lack the understanding of the theoretical foundation or principles that are the equivalent of college-level learning.

The process of petitioning for prior learning credit does not guarantee that credit is awarded. However, due to screening and advisement, many students are well equipped to earn college credit for what they know.

How Is This Book Organized?

This book is divided into four sections:

Part I: The Prior Learning Assessment Process

Chapters 1–4 provide an introduction to prior learning assessment, adult learner profiles, educational goal-setting, prior learning assessment planning, and standards for assessment.

Part II: Transcripts and Testing

Chapters 5 and 6 provide information on ways to obtain credit for transcripts and training (Chapter 5) and credit by examination (Chapter 6).

Part III: Portfolio Development

Chapters 7–11 provide a review of learning theory and the development of a portfolio of prior learning, which is the method of assessment that requires the most guidance.

The Appendices provide instructions on creating a prior learning inventory as well as resources, forms, samples, and definitions.

REVIEW

- Prior learning assessment can be a valuable complement to college coursework for adult students who are seeking a degree.
- Policies vary from college to college, so it is important to work closely with an academic advisor or prior learning assessment expert.
- Commonly used assessment methods include training and coursework evaluation, testing, and portfolio.

- The prior learning portfolio is a method used to demonstrate and evaluate a student's learning.
- The benefits of prior learning assessment include time, cost, career development, and critical thinking.

NEXT STEPS

1. Using the information provided in Appendix 1, conduct an Internet search for colleges that offer prior learning assessment services. Locate the policies for prior learning assessment used by the college you plan on attending.
2. Develop a prior learning inventory on your computer (see Appendix 2 for instructions). The inventory will be a useful resource for planning prior learning assessment.

REFERENCES

Adult Council on Education (ACE). Find an ACE-Reviewed Training Course Provider. Retrieved August 30, 2005, http://www.acenet.edu/AM/Template.cfm?Section=Organizational_Services&Template=/CM/HTMLDisplay.cfm&ContentID=6034.

Bahr, M. (October 2002). From Job Security to Career Mobility: The Importance of Lifelong Learning. Retrieved September 7, 2004, http://www.acenet.edu/clll/centerpoint/index.cfm?articleID=114.

Bureau of Labor Statistics, U.S. Department of Labor. *Occupational Outlook Handbook, 2004–05 Edition*. Retrieved August 30, 2005, http://www.bls.gov/oco/.

CAEL. Report to the National Commission on Accountability in Higher Education. Retrieved August 30, 2005, http://www.sheeo.org/account/comm/testim/CAEL%20testimony.pdf.

College Board. About CLEP. Retrieved August 30, 2005, http://www.collegeboard.com/student/testing/clep/about.html.

College Board. Colleges Granting CLEP Tests. Retrieved August 30, 2005, http://apps.collegeboard.com/cbsearch_clep/searchCLEPColleges.jsp.

Day, J.C., & Newburger, E.C. (2002). The Big Payoff: Educational Attainment and Synthetic Estimates of Work-Life Earnings. (Current Population Reports, Special Studies, P23–210). Washington, DC: Commerce Dept., Economics and Statistics Administration, Census Bureau. Retrieved August 30, 2005, http://www.census.gov/prod/2002pubs/p23-210.pdf.

Dow, G. Community College of Vermont. Retrieved September 7, 2004, http://www.ccv.edu/APL.

Kolb, D.A. (1984). *Experiential Learning.* New Jersey: Prentice Hall.

Lamdin, L. (1992). *Earn College Credit for What You Know.* Chicago: CAEL.

LeGrow, M., Sheckley, B., & Kehrhahn, M. (Fall 2002). Comparison of Problem-Solving Performance Between Adults Receiving Credit via Assessment of Prior Learning and Adults Completing Classroom Courses. *The Journal of Continuing Higher Education. 50* (3), 2–13.

Lumina Foundation. (2005). Adult Learners. Retrieved October 17, 2005, from http://www.luminafoundation.org/adult_learners/.

Voorhees, R. & Lingenfelter, P. (2003). Adult Learners and State Policy. Retrieved August 30, 2005, http://www.sheeo.org/workfrce/CAEL%20paper.pdf.

Whitaker, U. (1989). *Assessing Learning: Standards, Principles and Procedures.* Chicago: CAEL.

Zucker, B., Johnson, C., Flint, T. (1999). *Prior Learning Assessment: A Guidebook to American Institutional Practices.* Chicago: CAEL. Kendall/Hunt.

Zuckerman, M.B. (2004 March 8). A truly cruel college squeeze. *U.S. News and World Report*, 80.

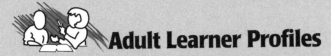# Adult Learner Profiles

Note to the Reader: The following profiles provide illustrations of adult learners who have successfully used prior learning assessment methods to earn college credit. In some cases, identifying information of the students, names of places where they worked, or their backgrounds have been altered to protect their confidentiality. The profiles represent actual students' experiences based on interviews. Andrew's profile is based on one student's experience. The profile of "Tim" is a composite of two students' experiences, both who majored in computer information science and attended the same college. The profile "Maria" is a composite of several students' experiences from two different colleges. In all cases, the profiles reflect the attitudes and experiences of real adult students who have earned college credit for what they know.

1. Adult learner profile: Andrew

Profession: Minister

Completed bachelor's degree in an adult learning program.

Obtained a bachelor's degree in liberal arts, with a minor in psychology.

Completed master of arts in communication studies. Currently pursuing doctorate.

Credits earned through prior learning assessment (semester hours awarded):

Portfolio:

Psychology: crisis intervention (2); pastoral psychology (2); human interaction skills (2); theories of personality (2)

Family and consumer science: death and dying (1)

English: the Bible as literature (2)

Communication: speech communication (3); video production (3); communication in families (3); small-group communication (3); advanced public speaking (3); communication and conflict (3); introduction to organizational communication (3)

Total credit hours petitioned: 39

Total credit hours awarded: 33

Pace: Andrew completed his portfolio in three months by working diligently on one portfolio essay per week.

Motivation: When Andrew's stepfather became disabled, he quit college to provide income for the family. Twenty years later, when Andrew returned to college, he felt comfortable attending courses with other working adults.

Process: Andrew attended a three-hour portfolio workshop offered by the college. After making a list of his skills and knowledge and comparing it with course syllabi, he had discussions with an advisor who helped him think about whether he could meet the course outcomes with his learning. In some cases, the discussions helped him target the best courses to match his learning.

Result: Seeking a degree seemed like a long and drawn-out process, so the portfolio provided him with an efficient means to finish. The essays (also known as narratives) allowed him to reflect on all he had learned, valued, and discovered in his work as a minister. Andrew said he became keenly aware of his tacit knowledge, that is, the depth and breadth of knowledge he had from experience. The process also proved valuable when taking course-work because he could add new knowledge and theory to his understanding.

Advice: "Just do it!" said Andrew, who is very persuasive about prior learning assessment. He advises students to stay focused on the task and put their primary attention toward getting the portfolio done. He says, "It is essential that you communicate with immediate family members that you will be preoccupied with your learning goals during this process. For example, my wife felt included because I had her proofread my papers. She was also helpful in confirming facts and timelines."

He adds, "I can't emphasize enough how much the reflective writing practice benefited me in my future coursework, including my graduate studies." Now after completing his master's degree, Andrew is pursuing a doctorate. (Interview with Robinson, A., personal communication, October 3, 2004)

2. Adult learner profile: Tim

Profession: software developer

Completed a bachelor of science in computer information science in a school for professional studies program.

Credits earned through prior learning assessment (semester hours awarded):

Credit by examination: Challenge exam (offered by the university): UNIX (3), CLEP: freshman college composition (6)

Portfolio: managing Internet information systems/Web development/e-mail (4); process mapping and process improvement (3); business writing (3); project management (3); leadership (0)

Total credit hours petitioned: 25

Total credit hours awarded: 22

Pace: Tim devoted approximately four months to reviewing for exams and preparing the portfolio.

Motivation: Tim described his motivation as twofold: the degree would give him leverage in a competitive market, and portfolio assessment would help him speed up the process of obtaining the degree. "After plodding along and taking four to six college classes [over] a period of 10 years, I wanted to get it done."

Process: Tim completed an online three-credit-hour prior learning assessment course to learn the portfolio method. Since the portfolio required extensive writing, he received reviews from the instructor and submitted his essays to an online writing lab for feedback. As an online student, Tim felt that receiving writing feedback electronically was less intimidating than in person. In addition, Tim prepared thoroughly for the challenge exam even though he did UNIX programming every day at work. Tim used his study time efficiently by reviewing commands he used less frequently.

Result: The combination of portfolio, credit by examination, transfer credit, and coursework allowed Tim to complete the exact number of credits he needed to graduate. Using prior learning assessment also helped him devote more time to the coursework he needed to learn.

Advice: "Stay organized," suggests Tim, who entered his tasks on a detailed project management spreadsheet. His game plan also involved gaining support from his boss in order to juggle his portfolio preparation and workload. Tim advises students to start the process early in their educational plan because, "I really killed myself at the end spending many late nights editing and completing my portfolio. I had to be creative in managing my time to complete this high volume of work." At his last performance appraisal, Tim was proud to tell his boss that he earned his bachelor's degree. (Interviews with Rhyne, T., personal communication, September 3, 2004, and Lee, T., personal communication, October 3, 2004)

3. Adult learner profile: Maria

Profession: early childhood education assistant, Head Start program

Maria completed her associate degree in early childhood education at a local community college. She is currently enrolled in a combined bachelor's/master's (B.S./M.A.) degree program in early childhood education/childhood education.

Credits earned through prior learning assessment (quarter hours awarded):

Credit by examination: CLEP: Spanish (6)

Portfolio: early childhood education methods (2); first aid (1); comparing cultures (2); introduction to communication (3); piano class I (3)

Total credit hours petitioned: 14

Total credit hours awarded: 11

Pace: The associate degree required completion of 105 credits during six quarters. Maria completed her portfolio one summer when she was mid-way through her studies.

Motivation: After many years of experience as a mother, educator for a non-profit organization, day care provider, and teacher of three-, four-, and five-year-old children, Maria wanted to learn more about her field and career and earn credit for her 13 years of working with children. Her short-term goal was to become a lead teacher at the Head Start program where she worked.

Process: First, Maria applied for admission at the community college she attended and took her placement assessment tests. Next, she completed her first three quarters of early childhood education courses in the traditional classroom. At that point, her advisor recommended that she enroll in the three-credit hour "Prior Learning Portfolio Development" course.

Result: The 11-week portfolio development course she completed gave her flexibility to work independently on the project. The combination of portfolio and CLEP testing allowed Maria to earn her elective and humanities credits and focus on her early childhood education coursework.

Advice: The goal-setting exercises and chronological record of her work and family experiences since high school helped Maria distinguish her learning from experience. After running a day care, working at a nonprofit organization, and attending numerous training sessions at the Head Start program where she worked, she found that it was valuable to stop and think about her lifelong learning. Collecting letters for documentation from former colleagues and clients took several weeks, but she was pleased when the letters arrived in her mailbox. Distinguishing learning from experience was at first challenging for Maria, but with the assistance of the faculty members who reviewed several drafts, she was able to strengthen her request for credit. "I'm so proud of my portfolio," says Maria, who stores her portfolio in a zippered leather case in the hope that one day she will show it to her grandchildren (Maria's profile is a composite of several students' experience).

CHAPTER 2

Determining Your Educational Goals

"Returning to school as an adult learner was scary at first. I was excited and nervous simultaneously. What I found was that I was respected for the life experience I brought into the classroom. We were encouraged as students to learn from one another and critically reflect on material. It became one of the most rewarding experiences of my life."

—KRIS, ADULT LEARNER WHO COMPLETED A PORTFOLIO COURSE

Why Should I Determine My Educational Goals?

The process of goal-setting helps students understand the link between career and educational goals. An educational goal is the driver that determines a student's selection of a college, major, coursework, and, subsequently, the plan for earning credit for prior learning. Therefore, clarifying the educational goal, and the motivation behind the goal, is a critical first step. Most adult students shoulder sole financial responsibility for their education, so they do not have the luxury of waiting a year or two to experiment with coursework before determining their goal.

In the corporate setting, clarifying goals helps team members build vision and momentum. Likewise, determining an educational goal helps students build momentum toward graduation. Goal-setting pushes students to exceed their previous accomplishments. Moreover, goal-setting gives students passion, energy, and drive when faced with obstacles. Simply stated, "The clearer your vision of what you seek, the closer you are to finding it" (Bolles, 2004, p. 128).

What If I Don't Know My Educational Goals?

Starting an education means taking steps from goal-setting to planning. If a student feels stuck in the goal-setting phase, it may be useful to consult a career counselor or join a career-development group. The old interest inventories many students took in high school are not the same caliber as the sophisticated inventories now available. In addition, many of the interest-and-skills assessments can be taken online at a low cost. The most effective results are found when assessment tools are used in combinations (such as the Strong Interest Inventory® and Myers Briggs Type Indicator®) and interpreted by a career counselor. Even if this consultation period delays the start of college, the time invested is valuable because it can help reinforce or even dramatically change a student's goal.

Career and educational exploration encourages adults to take actions and make well-informed decisions (see Box 2.1 below). Actions such as networking with experts are valuable because many careers such as forensic accounting did not exist even five years ago. Hastily made decisions are often less than satisfying. Also, some students jump into their education

BOX 2.1 Actions That Help Clarify Educational Goals

On the need to take action, Ibarra states, "We like to think that the key to a successful career change is knowing what we want to do next and then using that knowledge to guide our actions. But change usually happens the other way around: doing comes first, knowing second" (Ibarra, 2003, p. 1).

Actions may include:

1. conducting informational interviews
2. researching trends in the marketplace
3. setting aside one night a week to pursue an interest in a new field
4. joining a professional organization or attending one of their functions
5. volunteering in a new field
6. job-shadowing for a day or several days
7. asking permission and visiting a class at a college you are considering or taking an online class
8. joining online discussion groups, forums, and networking groups
9. researching information on financial aid options (such as corporate or military educational benefits, student loans, or grants)
10. investigating educational options

prematurely or after a particularly painful period or a life transition such as a divorce, death of a parent, or sudden empty nest, when they have not yet fully examined their options. According to one career counselor, many students spend more time shopping for a car than researching their career and educational goals even though they are making such a large investment in time and money.

Unfortunately, obtaining a degree does not guarantee a job or a promotion. Job trends show that many adults will work as independent contractors for companies rather than as long-term employees. Students should make the best educational decision possible, realizing that the job market shifts dramatically due to many unforeseen factors. Skills gained in college such as communication, critical thinking, managing projects, and working with diverse teams are valuable tools in a fluctuating economy.

How Do I Select a College?

Many colleges can fulfill the goal of providing a solid education. Therefore, it is a good idea to research every option available in a major or field of interest. Research can be conducted using the Internet and books and by making personal contacts. Most colleges, due to privacy issues, do not release contact information for students, so networking through professional organizations or online groups might be a better way to contact students or alumni. To narrow a college search, write a list of the most important criteria (see Box 2.2). Second, narrow the list to a few key factors and find several schools that match the criteria. Third, conduct thorough research of the selections. Take into consideration that many private colleges are affordable when combined with prior learning assessment.

What Is Distance Learning?

Distance learning—also known as online study, distance education, or distributed learning—relies on educational technologies such as the Internet, CDs, or video for delivery. With the availability of the Internet and the low cost of computers, many students are benefiting from taking courses online. According to the University Continuing Education Association, "The International Data Corporation predicts that by 2005, 90 percent of all higher education institutions will have e-learning programs" (2002, p. 71).

When taking courses online, students typically enter a password-protected site, which allows them to view the course materials, assignments, instructor's messages, and classmates' threaded discussions. Students may post messages at any time during the day or night, but they must adhere to

BOX 2.2 Criteria for Selecting a College

Develop a list of the criteria you will use for selecting a college. Your list may include:

- Major, minor, or certificate offered
- Accreditation (see Appendix 3)
- Coursework and instructors who bring real-life learning into the classroom
- Availability of required courses in major (view course schedules)
- Availability of online, distance, or individualized courses
- Cost
- Prior learning assessment options, services, and potential cost savings
- Time to completion
- Preparation for graduate work
- Convenience
- Learning preferences (classroom-based or online instruction)
- Financial aid, loan, or fee-deferment options
- Convenience of student services such as computer labs, library services, child care, and career counseling (see Box 2.3)
- Accessibility and services for the disabled
- Transferability of coursework
- Other (fill in factors)

deadlines for posting their ideas to the discussion and handing in assignments. Many students are surprised that the discussions are lively, social, and educational. The growth of online learning has also resulted in a tremendous variety of student backgrounds—including students who are stationed in military bases overseas, seniors who don't want to go to classes at night, students with mobility limitations, and students from other countries.

How Long Will It Take to Earn a Degree?

The length of time will depend on the goal and the amount of credit a student has previously obtained. On the whole, it is important that students set out to receive the maximum benefits from their education. But focusing on a quick fix often results in missing the richest learning opportunities. As Mike Zizzi, a seasoned communications professor, writes, "At the heart of adult learning, especially that offered in accelerated formats, is the stretching out

BOX 2.3 Adult-Friendly Colleges

Consider colleges that provide services for the adult learner such as:

- Flexible courses: evening and weekend classes, independent studies, accelerated and online courses
- Admission requirements that require work experience or training
- Academic advising and other support services offered during evening hours
- Prior learning assessment
- Majors designed to support marketplace needs
- Faculty with experience in the field and trained in adult learning models
- Coursework that emphasizes "real-world" experience and application
- Easy access to services

of time. For the adult learner, the course 'begins,' retrospectively, at the time of the student's earliest relevant experiences and the class 'ends' . . . well, at best, it never ends; the term may end and the final work may be turned in, but the learning continues to unfold" (2003, p. 359). Zizzi instructs adult students not to race through their programs of study but to work steadily toward realistic learning goals. To rush students during this important, self-rewarding part of life, Zizzi advises, cheats students of much of the benefits of education.

What Roadblocks Do Adult Learners Commonly Face?

One of the most common challenges is effective time management, especially when juggling several responsibilities such as finances, work, family, friendships, aging parents, household duties, and recreation. Before starting coursework, it can be insightful to complete at least one time-management exercise (see Box 2.4). After all, anything worth doing, including an education, takes time.

Ineffective time management can lead to another roadblock—procrastination, the habit of neglecting to complete tasks that need to be accomplished. Procrastination can result in falling behind on assignments, increased stress, and rushed work. Most students suffer from procrastination to some degree, but there are brilliant procrastinators, who, once they start to lag

BOX 2.4 Time-Management Activities

Option 1: Time-management chart

1. Create a handwritten or computer-generated table that lists your waking hours (such as 6–7 a.m., 7–8 a.m.).
2. Fill in the slotted times with the activities that you did during each hour. Ideally, keep track of your tasks for several days.
3. Using the information you collect, determine realistically where you could devote ten or more hours a week to your education. Also, determine your top ten time wasters.

Option 2: Take action

1. Brainstorm a list of creative options for using your time effectively such as riding a bus or train so you can do coursework, using an online grocery-delivery service, or reading or listening to tapes while working out on exercise equipment.
2. Try out one or two of your options to see if they are feasible.

Option 3: Duties and responsibilities

1. List the responsibilities and duties you have each week, even small responsibilities.
2. Determine which of your responsibilities only you can do and cross those out. From your remaining list, determine responsibilities that you could live without, live with less attention, or delegate to someone else.

behind, can't catch up. Researching strategies to deal with procrastination and testing the strategies can be useful before the stakes are high.

In addition to time-management challenges, many adult learners feel they have rusty skills. Students who know that their skills are rusty might brush up on study skills, writing, reading, math, and computer skills before starting coursework. Even learning simple techniques such as prewriting strategies and mind mapping can help avoid keyboard block, a form of writing block characterized by staring at a blank screen. Many community colleges and community adult education programs offer low-cost or free workshops and labs with computer programs to help students get up to speed. The atmosphere in the labs is friendly and nonthreatening. Also, many labs are often fully equipped to help students who have learned English as a second language. Finally, many adult-oriented colleges offer introductory courses to help new students prepare for the challenges ahead.

There are additional steps that students can take to get the maximum benefit from their college experience. One step might involve setting up an office in the home or finding a workstation that is quiet, comfortable, ergonomic, and has good lighting. Another step might involve determining the hardware and software requirements as well as the computer skills needed to be successful, especially if considering online courses. Even scheduling an eye examination can be a valuable step because of the intensive reading and computer work required.

Finishing an education is a large undertaking; accordingly, it is important to discuss plans with family members and co-workers. One report showed that "two key persistence risk factors are work intensity and family responsibility" (ACE, 2003, p. 3). Negotiating ways to lessen workload with employers, if at all feasible, is a good idea. The decision to return to school has an effect on family members such as spouses, significant others, children, and stepchildren, so it is best to move ahead only with their enthusiastic support. Many of the roadblocks that adult learners encounter, if anticipated, can be addressed.

What Are Some Tips for Writing My Educational Goals?

Examine goals and motivation.

Students should determine their goals and the motivation—the reasons that they are pursuing the goal. In the book *Good to Great*, Jim Collins (2001) states that passion and motivation in companies or individuals can't be manufactured, "If you become the best at something, you'll never remain on top if you don't have an intrinsic passion for what you are doing" (p. 97). Research has shown that students work longer and with more intensity when they are motivated than when they are not, especially when they face obstacles. Wlodkowski writes, "When we match two people of identical ability and give them the identical opportunity and conditions to achieve, the motivated person will surpass the unmotivated person in performance and outcome" (1999, p. 4).

Use writing and learning style strengths and preferences.

Students benefit from using their preferences for approaching writing tasks. Some write concisely and have no trouble adding a lot of detail, so they may benefit from first answering some of the questions to narrow their thoughts.

Other writers tend to take many divergent trails of thought and, in the process, are able to narrow the ideas. Learners who prefer to process ideas aloud might want to have conversations with several good listeners before writing down their educational goals. Visual learners might start by drawing a mind map (on paper or electronically) to visualize webs of ideas, or they might create a collage of ideas from magazines. Learners who need peace and quiet for reflection might take a walk or a one-day retreat to help clarify their goals. In addition, according to Ronald Gross, everyone has peaks and valleys of learning times during the day, so it may help to clear some time during the most productive times of the day to write (1999, p. 85).

Review and revise goals periodically.

A good educational goal statement is revisited and changed from time to time. Many adult students report that they initially returned to college out of the desire to make more money and receive a promotion. However, as they successfully passed classes and interacted with instructors, they refined their motivation to include the opportunity to learn, examine larger perspectives, meet people from other countries, and challenge their views.

BOX 2.5   Educational Goal Questions

Using the following questions to help you get started, write your educational goal. You can write several pages or a short synopsis, but the clearer and more specific, the better.

Goal, Motivation, and Time Frame
- What is your goal?
- Where and when will you attend college?
- What are the reasons (professional and personal) you are pursuing your goal?
- What is a realistic timeframe for completing your education?

Looking Back
- Was there a turning point when you reached the decision to return to school?
- What are the changes that you've witnessed in the workplace, your personal life, and society that have had an effect on your decision to return to school?

(continued)

- What are your thoughts and feelings about not having finished your education?

Looking Forward
- What assets do you bring to the classroom that you did not have even five to ten years ago?
- What combinations of emotions do you have as you think about returning to school (such as fear and excitement)?
- Where do you see your career headed in the next five to ten years?
- How would you feel if you do not achieve your educational goal?

Action Plan
- What is your plan to receive the maximum benefit from your education?
- What changes in your lifestyle are you able to make in order to find time for class work?
- What are several action steps that you can take now that will help you manage your time effectively?
- Who will support you in pursuing your goal?
- Are there any skills you need to be better prepared for the challenges ahead, and if so, how will you brush up on those skills?

 **Adult Learner Profile**

Maria's educational goal (excerpt):

> *My twin boys are now 14 years old, and I've worked with young children since they were born. If I want my boys to be more serious about their education, I need to lead by example. I admire the lead teachers at the Head Start program where I work because I know the program makes a difference in children's literacy. My parents worked hard in the onion fields and never finished high school. I am determined to finish my associate of arts degree and then enroll in a program where I can complete my bachelor's and even a master's degree. I know it's never too late to learn.*

REVIEW

- Setting educational goals is the first step in prior learning assessment.
- Time spent in career planning and researching colleges helps students make well-informed decisions.
- When writing educational goal statements, the clearer and more specific, the better.

NEXT STEPS

1. Write your educational goal.
2. Investigate several options for clarifying your educational goals.
3. Try time-management activities to discover your biggest time savers and time wasters.
4. Start a "to-do" list with your admissions tasks such as filing an application, requesting transcripts, and completing assessments.

REFERENCES

American Council on Education Center for Policy Analysis. (2003, August). Student success: Understanding Graduation and Persistence Rates. *ACE Issue Brief.* Retrieved September 20, 2004, http://www.acenet.edu/programs/policy.

Bolles, R.N. (2004). *What Color Is Your Parachute?* Berkeley, CA: Ten Speed Press.

Collins, J. (2001). *Good to Great.* New York: Harper Business Books.

Gross, R. (1999). *Peak Learning.* New York, NY: Putman.

Ibarra, H. (2003). *Working Identity: Unconventional Strategies for Reinventing Your Career.* Boston, MA: Harvard Business School Press.

UCEA. (2002). University Continuing Education Association Commission on Quality Issues Paper. Washington, DC: UCEA.

Wlodkowski, R.J. (1998). *Enhancing Adult Motivation to Learn: A Comprehensive Guide for Teaching All Adults.* San Francisco, CA: Jossey-Bass Publishers.

Zizzi, M.P. (2003). Successful Communication for Adult Learners. In *Adult Learning.* Boston: Pearson.

ADDITIONAL RESOURCES

www.petersons.com
Provides information on colleges and universities, adult learning, distance programs, financial aid, test preparation, and career preparation. Students should be aware that some colleges advertise on the site.

www.jobhuntersbible.com

Online resources that accompany Richard Bolles' book *What Color Is Your Parachute?*

www.careerjournal.com

Career site with articles that address the needs of working professionals published by the *Wall Street Journal.*

CHAPTER 3

Prior Learning Assessment and Coursework Planning

"Without a plan, a dream is just wishful thinking."

—GRAHAM COOKE, CONFERENCE SPEAKER AND AUTHOR

"I completed and was awarded 24 hours of credit through portfolio and testing. I transferred in a considerable amount of credits; otherwise, I would have planned to complete more credit through prior learning assessment."

-KRISTI, AN ADULT LEARNER

Why Do I Need a Plan?

Adults who return to college come to the table with a variety of credits, training, and learning experiences that add complexity to determining their educational plans. The degree is the most critical document students will need to meet their educational goals. Planning helps students identify all of the options available to them and creates a process whereby students can effectively and efficiently complete their educational goals. This plan guides all of a student's decisions regarding coursework and prior learning assessment methods. Jumping into prior learning assessment or coursework without a plan can result in paying for credit not needed or taking a course for which they may have been able to earn credit.

Planning also helps students complete their education at a reasonable pace. One faculty advisor, Margo Rosenkranz, states, "It is important that PLA be woven into the tapestry of the entire degree plan and career path. It is wise to view PLA as a valid means to an end, but not solely as a way to reduce the cost of a college education or a quick method of acquiring credit. Proper planning helps students build a meaningful educational experience" (personal communication, July 1, 2005).

Who Will Assist Me in Mapping Out My Educational Plan?

Degree or coursework planning is completed with assistance from advisors, who are also known as academic advisors, degree plan specialists, faculty mentors, or prior learning assessment specialists. Advisors are normally assigned after a student completes the admission process and sends official copies of transcripts to the college (see Chapter 5). Advisors may be available on a drop-in basis, by e-mail, or by telephone. An advisor is highly trained to understand the sequence of courses, transfer policies, course loads, and prior learning options (see Box 3.1).

BOX 3.1 Meeting with Academic Advisors

Students should not rely solely on the advice of other students or information on Web sites to make educational planning decisions. When meeting with advisors, it is important to:

1. Compile degree-planning information. Review the student handbook (paper or electronic) regarding majors, courses offered, and requirements. Print out or bring copies of any checklists of requirements and student records. Bring a copy of the inventory, which helps students remember their previous education, training, and knowledge that may be relevant to degree planning (see Appendix 2). This inventory can help the academic advisor understand the student's prior learning.

2. Communicate effectively
   - In person, be prepared to ask questions, take notes, and write answers.
   - By e-mail, write a detailed and numbered list of questions. Include full name, program, and student identification number.
   - By phone, identify full name, student identification number, phone numbers, and available times to talk.

3. Verify transfer credits and course options. Course substitutions or waivers require an advisor's approval.

What Questions Should I Ask about Prior Learning Assessment (PLA)?

The following questions can be discussed with an advisor, or the questions may be answered by attending a PLA course or workshop.

BOX 3.2 PLA Questions

PLA Methods

What prior learning assessment options are available?

- Portfolio assessment
- Credit by examination (CLEP, DSST, challenge exams, etc.)
- Is there a list of course equivalencies for these exams?
- ACE recommendation on training, certifications, and military education
- Other methods of assessment

Procedures:

- When can I start earning PLA credits (After I am enrolled? After I have completed coursework?)
- When can I enroll in a prior learning assessment class, workshop, or program (if offered)?
- Is it advisable to take a writing course first?
- Is there a deadline for completing PLA credits (before graduation)?

Fees:

- What are the fees?
- Where do I pay the fees?

Who:

- Whom should I contact to discuss PLA options?
- Who will evaluate the portfolio?

Where:

- Location of samples of student portfolios available to review?
- Location of handouts or resources?
- Does the college serve as a CLEP or DSST testing center? If not, where is the closest authorized testing center located?

(continued)

- Is there a limit on the number of total credits a student can earn through PLA?
- What factors influence the limit (such as a residency requirement)?
- To which section of the degree program can the PLA credit be applied (general studies, major, minor, electives)? Is there a limit on the number of PLA credits that can be earned in each category, or in the upper level or lower level?
- Which courses are not eligible for PLA credit (seminars, capstone projects, internships)?
- Does the college follow the CAEL recommended standards for assessment (outlined in Chapter 4)?
- Is there a penalty for failing an assessment?
- What areas or subject matter are most commonly petitioned?
- How many credits, on average, do students earn through PLA?

What Factors Should I Consider When Mapping Out a Plan?

When mapping an educational plan, determine all the coursework and assessment options available. After determining the credits needed, make informed decisions based on the following factors (see Box 3.3).

BOX 3.3 Factors to Consider in Educational Planning

Quality of education
Consider ways to maximize the learning opportunity by taking a wide range of courses or examinations across the disciplines while developing mastery in the major or field.

Course offerings
Consider how courses are offered. Are they offered at a time, at a place, or using a method that allows students to participate?

(continued)

Sequencing

Consider the sequence of the course. For instance, there may be fundamental or prerequisite courses that need to be taken before enrolling in another course. If needed, plan on taking review courses in such areas as writing or math.

Cost

Consider the cost savings of using testing or portfolio-assisted assessment.

Time

Schedule time wisely to avoid overload. Since building a quality portfolio is worthwhile and takes time, schedule the activity when coursework is light.

Prior learning assessment options

Consider that during the portfolio assessment process, many students are surprised to uncover how much learning they could use to petition for credit. Therefore, the plan should be flexible enough to allow students who discover ways to earn credit through prior learning assessment.

Preferred learning style

Consider learning preferences. Determine the best fit. If a student prefers face-to-face or hands-on instruction, he or she should consider ground-based courses. At the same time, don't place limitations on using distance-education options. Many students are surprised at the quality of instruction and discussion available on online forums.

Accreditation

Consider the type of accreditation the school holds. Accreditation may be a factor for students who transfer credit (e.g., credits from a technical college may not transfer to a regionally accredited liberal arts college).

Graduate studies

Consider plans for graduate studies and the need for prerequisite coursework.

What Are the Components of a Typical Bachelor's Degree Program?

General or core requirements: Also known as general education (gen-ed), general studies, university studies, core requirements, core curriculum, or group studies. These requirements may include but are not limited to: English, math, natural sciences, humanities, and social sciences. Other requirements may include religious studies or philosophy, computer technology, or international/global studies.

Major: Student's primary area of academic concentration. Includes lower-division or lower-level (generally 100–200 level) and upper-division or upper-level credit (300–400 level) coursework.

Minor: Normally a minor is completed with four or more courses in an area of study. In most bachelor's degree programs, minors are optional.

Electives: Also known as general electives, open electives, or free electives. Used to place any course that is not required by the major or core studies.

How Can I Use Prior Learning Assessment Methods to Meet Degree Requirements?

The following examples illustrate how three students used a combination of methods to fulfill bachelor's and associate degree requirements (see Box 3.4).

**Adult Learner Profiles**

BOX 3.4   Mapping Credits

Andrew
Goal: Bachelor of arts degree in liberal arts, minor in psychology

CREDITS	CATEGORY	NOTES
0	Transfer	Completed courses at a Bible college that did not transfer because the college was not regionally accredited. Experience identified by advisor as potential for portfolio evaluation.
33	Portfolio	Combined his pastoral and communication experience and knowledge of communication principles to petition for credit.
87	Coursework	B.A. in liberal arts, minor in psychology
120	Total credits needed based on Semester Hours	

Tim
Goal: Bachelor of science degree in computer science

CREDITS	CATEGORY	NOTES
31	Transfer	Transferred credit from three different colleges. Credit that earned a "C minus" or higher grade was transferred. Credit earned at a technical college transferred as general elective credit (not credit in the major).
14	Military service	Training/service in the U.S. Army
3	Challenge Exam	UNIX
6	CLEP exam	"Freshman College Composition"
22	Portfolio	Combined his business and computer experience to petition for credit. (A maximum of 45 credits could be earned through portfolio at this college.)
1	College evaluation of certification (ACE evaluation)	Microsoft 2002 Office Specialist Certification
51	Coursework	B.S. in computer information science
128	Total credits needed based on Semester Hours	

(continued)

Maria
Goal: Associate of arts degree in early childhood education

CREDITS	CATEGORY	NOTES
11	Portfolio	Fulfilled a block of credit for portfolio based on work and training. (A maximum of 16 credits could be earned through portfolio at this college.)
6	CLEP Exam	"College Level Spanish Language"
88	Coursework	A.A. in early childhood education
105	Total credits needed based on Quarter Hours	

How Can I Use Prior Learning Assessment to Fulfill Elective Credit?

The elective category is the most flexible category for exploring prior learning assessment credit possibilities. Some degree plans or majors have more course requirements, leaving little room for general or free electives. Other plans allow 35 or more credits in the elective category. Since the elective category allows more freedom in the selection of courses, it may be an ideal area to fill with prior learning options.

To create a plan to fulfill general electives, simply start a list of the number of electives needed and the options for earning elective requirements such as coursework, military, training, transfer (covered in Chapter 5), portfolio (covered in Chapters 7–11), and credit by examination (covered in Chapter 6). Always double-check that the credits earned are not duplicated. Add up the number of credits earned in each category, as shown in Box 3.5.

Work with an academic advisor to first identify how many electives you need for your degree.

BOX 3.5   Charting Electives

Sample: Tim

CATEGORIES	CREDITS
Military	14
Training	1
Portfolio	4
Transfer	4
Total electives needed	23

How Can I Use Prior Learning Assessment to Fulfill General or Core Requirements?

It may be more difficult to use PLA options to meet core requirements than general electives. Core requirement categories such as English, math, social science, and humanities have greater restrictions. One way to map out the options for fulfilling general or core requirements is to create a table (see Box 3.6 for directions).

BOX 3.6   General or Core Requirements Preliminary Worksheet

Instructions:

1. Create a table or a spreadsheet. List the core course requirements and number of credits needed to fulfill. Indicate the courses fulfilled by transfer.

2. Take careful notes from meetings with advisors on options eligible to meet each requirement. If using a spreadsheet or table, double or triple the size of the boxes.

3. Note acceptable exams or portfolio options related to a student's prior learning.

4. Check that courses are not duplicated—that is, are not used in more than one slot.

(continued)

 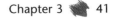

5. Verify all prior learning assessment options with an advisor or portfolio specialist.

6. Use the chart as a process of discovery. The decisions may need adjustment as students uncover their learning during the portfolio assessment process.

7. Construct a timeline for completing prior learning assessment credit.

Background: The student who created this worksheet (Box 3.7) had experience in crisis counseling, interviewing, and organizational development at several nonprofit organizations, so she noted the exams and portfolio options related to her prior learning. There were many more options available than listed in this chart, but working on a preliminary plan was valuable to the learner to help map out the options she did not previously consider.

Assessment options depend on an individual's learning experiences and how the learning relates to college-level learning.

How Can I Use Prior Learning Assessment Methods to Fulfill Major or Minor Requirements?

Students must understand their college's policies. In some cases, students can use prior learning assessment credits to fulfill major or minor requirements. However, there are likely to be more restrictions in this category. For instance, prior learning assessment credits may be restricted to fulfilling half of the total credits needed for a minor. Students with extensive experiential learning may have a strong practical understanding of the topic, but they may be limited in their theoretical understanding. Theoretical understanding helps students place their applied learning in a larger context and helps build a strong foundation of understanding for future coursework. Some colleges offer short theory-building courses to students that, when combined with their prior learning, can fulfill course requirements. Ultimately, prior learning assessment is intended to help students measure what they know without compromising their learning in a chosen field. Therefore, students should seek the advice of advisors or faculty members when petitioning for credit in their major.

BOX 3.7 Core Requirements Sample Worksheet

CATEGORY (FILL IN THE REQUIREMENTS REQUIRED)	# OF CREDITS NEEDED	ACCEPTABLE COURSES OR COURSE DISCIPLINES	ACCEPTABLE EXAMS RELATED TO MY PRIOR LEARNING	POSSIBLE PORT-FOLIO PETITIONS RELATED TO MY PRIOR LEARNING	PRELIMINARY DECISIONS VERIFIED BY MY ADVISOR (SEE ✓)
English	6	Transferred English credits from a community college.✓			
Mathematics	3	Math—college algebra and above. Take math assessment first.	None	None	Take statistics course✓
Social science	6	Psychology, economics, history, sociology	"Human Growth & Development " (CLEP), "Fund of Counseling" (DTTS)	Organizational psychology, Crisis theory and practice, Interviewing	Take portfolio course and discuss options with instructor.✓
International studies	6	Language, global studies	French (CLEP)		Review French and try CLEP exam.✓
Natural science	3	Transferred astronomy course from a community college.✓			
Philosophy and religion	6	Philosophy, religion	None	None	Take courses.✓
Humanities	6	Communication, English, humanities	"Analyzing and Interpreting Literature" (CLEP)	Interviewing theory and practice	Interested in expanding my love of literature and will take courses.✓

Continue chart for additional requirements.
✓ Checked with advisor.

BOX 3.8 Considerations when Fulfilling Coursework in the Major or Minor

Sequencing
Foundation courses help students build a solid understanding for future courses. Sequencing is especially important in fields such as nursing or computer science, where the sequence of learning is essential and, if missed, may hinder a student's success.

Levels of theory and expertise required
Students may consult a professor in their chosen discipline to help determine whether their prior learning is at the level and depth that is equivalent to college-level courses in the major or minor.

Plans for graduate school
Some graduate schools may require that a specific number of credits be completed through coursework, so it is worth checking their policy if graduate school is being considered.

REVIEW

- Creating a plan with the help of an advisor helps students to avoid earning more credit than needed to meet their goal.
- There are no ironclad rules for determining where prior learning assessment applies. Students should research all their options and make decisions based on prior learning assessment, quality of education, time, cost, preferred learning style, and sequencing.
- Adult learners bring a variety of learning experiences that can be used successfully to fulfill a variety of degree requirements without compromising learning in their chosen field.
- Meeting with a prior learning specialist or taking a course or workshop in portfolio-assisted assessment early in a student's educational program will help students set the stage for future course planning.

NEXT STEPS

1. Determine the policies and guidelines for using prior learning assessment methods.
2. Research and create a spreadsheet of degree requirements and options.
3. Start a list of questions or create a preliminary chart of options to verify with an academic advisor or prior learning specialist.

CHAPTER 4

CAEL Standards for the Assessment of Credit

This chapter provides information on the standards, principles, and procedures established by the Council for Adult and Experiential Learning (CAEL) for the governance of prior learning assessment. While these standards are written for college administrators and policy-makers, by reviewing the standards, students can appreciate that prior learning assessment is not a trendy "get credit quick" movement, but a well-established practice recognized by the most rigorous accrediting associations. Once more, students can gain insight on the policies colleges have established in order to maintain high standards for awarding credit for learning. Becoming familiar with the CAEL standards will help students determine quality programs.

What Are the Ten CAEL Standards for Assessment?

The following guidelines are published in the book *Assessing Learning: Standards, Principles and Procedures* (Whitaker, 1989, p. 9).

Standards relevant to the assessment process:

1. Credit should be awarded only for learning and not for experience.
2. College credit should be awarded only for college-level learning.
3. Credit should be awarded only for learning that has a balance, appropriate to the subject, between theory and practical application.
4. Competence levels and credit awards must be made by subject matter/academic experts.
5. Credit should be appropriate to the academic context in which it is accepted.

Standards used by colleges to set policies on awarding credit:

6. Credit awards and transcript entries should be monitored to avoid duplicating credit.
7. Policies and procedures (including appeals) should be fully disclosed and prominently available.
8. Fees charged for assessment should be based on services, not amount of credit.
9. Personnel involved in assessment should receive adequate training.
10. Assessment programs should be regularly monitored, reviewed, evaluated, and revised.

The following provides a further explanation of the standards.

1. Credit is awarded only for learning, and not for experience. What is the difference between learning and experience?

Experience is considered "an excellent potential source of learning," but experience alone is not considered an adequate yardstick for assessment (Whitaker, 1989, p. 11). The assessment of learning is not a simple calculation based on input—the hours or years spent in experience. Instead, it is based on the learning outcome. In fact, seat time in a class or number of years of experience in a job is not an accurate predictor of learning. In other words, a portfolio assessment shows that a student can demonstrate that learning was applied. Since the distinction between learning and experience is critical to the field of assessment, Chapter 7 provides an explanation of the difference between experience alone and experiential learning.

2. College credit is awarded only for college-level learning. What methods are used to determine whether learning is college level?

First, the learning must have been acquired after high school to be considered college level.

Second, the learning must be comparable to college-level courses, a distinction that is made by academic experts. The student's knowledge and skills need to match the level of learning typically taught in a college course. Certainly, adults have many valuable learning experiences such as fixing a home, negotiating a contract, or collecting antiques, yet that knowledge alone is not considered the equivalent of college-level coursework.

Likewise, students with significant learning from family experiences such as death and dying, divorce, aging, or child-rearing face more difficulty matching their learning to a college course because of the level of depth and breadth required in college to gain a full understanding and appreciation for the subject matter and theory. To demonstrate a full understanding of the subject matter, perhaps the student read books on the subject, attended workshops, or had discussions with experts.

Third, the learning must be transferable to several contexts or settings that a student might encounter. When assigning credit, every college has the freedom to design an evaluation form, which an evaluator or team of evaluators can use to write comments and indicate if the learning is college level as well as to determine the number and level of credits earned. The measure for awarding credits for prior learning is generally whether a student learned at a level of competence, which is usually considered a C minus (or 70 percent) or higher grade.

3. Credit is awarded only for learning that has a balance, appropriate to the subject, between theory and practical application. How does this standard apply to assessment?

Credit is granted for students who demonstrate a mix of theory and practical education appropriate to the course. According to Whitaker, the assessment process is shortchanged when it does not represent that balance. He states, "The learning is not complete until the learner has some understanding of what both the theory and the practical experience mean. It isn't enough to have both in isolation; the learner needs to know why they are necessary, and how each extends the value of the other" (1989, p. 14).

Some subject matters taught in college are heavily weighted toward practical experience and experimentation; others are heavily weighted toward theory. An introduction to business software applications requires considerable demonstration of skills learned in a computer lab, so the course has a large dose of practical application. Therefore, the student would have to prove a practical application of the skills to pass the class. An introductory course in Web design might have a mix of both theory and practical application because it covers principles for effective communication on the Web, but the principles are also directly applied.

A course in the methods of elementary education might have a balance between theory and practical application. For instance, the course may draw from direct experience in a classroom but may also incorporate educational theories and an awareness of multiculturalism. As illustrated in Box 4.1, an education course may require a balance of theory and application.

BOX 4.1 Balance between Theory and Practical Application

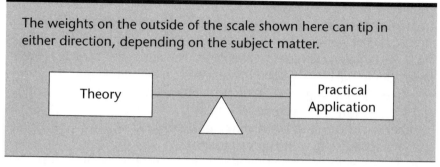

The weights on the outside of the scale shown here can tip in either direction, depending on the subject matter.

Theory   Practical Application

It follows that some courses are heavily weighted toward theory, definitions, ideas, and concepts, which is sometimes called book knowledge. Courses in such areas as history, philosophy, literature, and sociology may draw heavily from reading, understanding terms, and critical thinking. Therefore, these courses would weigh more heavily toward the theoretical side of the scale.

The point is that courses heavy in theory may be better assessed through examinations or through coursework because they can measure a student's theoretical knowledge. In addition, these courses may be difficult to petition using the portfolio method because of the difficulty of providing supporting documentation. For instance, a class like "Business Report Writing" is more easily demonstrated through the portfolio method; "Survey of English Literature before 1800," on the other hand, is better assessed through exam or by passing the course. In addition, courses that are considered upper level (normally 300 level or higher), may have a higher expectation for theory and, therefore, may require more depth of knowledge and application than a lower-level course (100–200 level). According to one faculty expert, it is the expectation that a student seeking prior learning credit "will have been exposed to the theory and to the corresponding literature within a subject area such that they can understand, reason, and explain to others the problems, choices, and decisions that are the content of a particular subject" (University of Wisconsin Green Bay, 2004).

4. The determination of competence levels and of credit awards is made by appropriate subject matter and academic experts. Who makes the credit determination?

Trained academic experts—normally faculty members on the campus—determine the level and number of credits awarded. Examinations (national and university-specific) are evaluated by academic committees that set standards for passing scores. Many colleges use blind assessment procedures to evaluate credit through portfolio, meaning that students don't know who will be evaluating their credit until the assessment is completed. On occasion, a college will consult faculty experts outside the campus to make credit determinations. The bottom line is that experts who determine credit awards are competent and trained in their field of expertise, so students cannot "fake it" by filling up the petition with jargon hoping to cover up inadequate learning.

5. Credit is appropriate to the academic context in which it is accepted. Why is this important?

This standard is a safeguard to help students who are petitioning for credit—students must specify how the credit for prior learning contributes to the degree or objective. As shown in Chapter 3, credits earned by assessment are carefully slotted to meet unfilled areas in the student's program of study. If a student decides to change his or her major course of study, prior learning assessment credits may need readjusting. Assessment is useful for academic planning because students look both backward to identify their past learning and forward to integrate that learning into their goal (Whitaker, 1989).

6. Credit awards and their transcript entries are monitored to avoid giving credit twice for the same learning. Why are credits monitored?

Monitoring of credits earned is essential to avoid duplication or "double-dipping" by earning the same credit twice. For example, a student who has received credit for a college-level English course would duplicate credit by taking the corresponding English CLEP examination. A course completed in "Supervisory Theory and Practice" might duplicate an exam in "Introduction to Supervision." If two or more course titles suggest redundancies, the student may need to obtain course descriptions or course syllabi to verify that the content of the courses was different.

7. Policies and procedures applied to assessment, including provision for appeal, should be fully disclosed and prominently available. Where are policies normally found?

Polices regarding prior learning assessment and credit by examination are published in the school's catalogue and, in many cases, published on the Web site. Or, prior learning assessment policies may be located in a PLA office. Students can contact the registrar's office or prior learning assessment office for policies.

8. Fees charged for assessment are based on the services performed in the process and are not determined by the amount of credit awarded. How does this standard affect me?

Fees for assessment are required up front. Additional fees may be required to transcript the credit or place the credit officially with the college's registrar. If submitting a portfolio of prior learning, fees are based on number of credits being petitioned, not the number of credits awarded. Paying the assessment fee is not a guarantee of credit.

9. Personnel involved in assessment should receive adequate training. Why is this standard important?

This standard assures the student of quality control. Since assessment is a complex process, colleges train staff and instructors to help guide students in the process.

10. Assessment programs should be regularly monitored, reviewed, evaluated, and revised. How does this standard affect me?

Assessment standards and policies are subject to change, so when applying for credit, it is important to double-check and follow the latest policy.

REVIEW

- The guidelines set by CAEL provide standards for quality control of assessment practices. Colleges set individual policies based on the standards.
- Credit is awarded based on the assessment of a student's learning and level of competence.
- The assessment process is shortchanged when it does not represent the balance appropriate to the course between theory and practical application.

NEXT STEPS

1. Locate and review the policies and procedures for prior learning assessment at your college. Compare the school's policies to the CAEL standards.

2. Locate course descriptions and, if available, course outcomes (the results of the learning) from college classes that closely match areas of your learning. What is your best estimate of the balance of theory and practical application required for the course (see also standard #3)?

REFERENCES

University of Wisconsin Green Bay. Credit for Prior Learning: Words of Wisdom from Faculty Reviewers. Retrieved August 20, 2004, http://www.uwgb.edu/assessment/CPL.htm.

Whitaker, U. (1989). *Assessing Learning: Standards, Principles and Procedures.* Chicago: CAEL.

ADDITIONAL RESOURCES

http://tip.psychology.org/
Explorations in Learning & Instruction: The Theory into Practice Database
TIP is an easy-to-navigate site that contains a database with brief summaries of 50 major theories of learning and instruction. The hyperlinks make connections between specific theories or to concepts that underlie a number of college disciplines.

http://www.maricopa.edu/academic/curric/
Maricopa Community College
Complete listing of courses offered by the Maricopa Community College with the competencies related to each college-level course. Search by discipline or by course.

PART

II

Transcripts and Testing

CHAPTER **5**

Evaluation of Transcripts and Training

What Does This Chapter Cover, and Why?

This chapter provides an overview of obtaining transcripts and training, including:

- Transcripts of college credit from colleges or universities (full or part time)
- Transcripts of military service and education
- Transcripts by ACE (American Council on Education)
- Training or examination records not certified by ACE

Obtaining transcripts of previous college work, military experience, certifications, or training is one of the first steps in the educational planning process.

What Are College Course Transcripts and How Do I Request Official Copies?

A college transcript is an official document from a college that lists the names and dates of courses taken, grades received, overall grade point average, and number of credits earned. Students should obtain official transcripts from previous college work as early as possible to start the admissions process (see Box 5.1). Some students make their decision to attend the college that accepts the most transfer credit, but that should just be one consideration when choosing the right institution.

It is important to obtain transcripts from every college attended, even if the transcript shows several bad grades. As part of the transcription process, the college sifts through the records and considers only the courses that meet standards for transfer credit. Past behavior is not a predictor of future success in college, especially with adult learners.

BOX 5.1   Official and Unofficial Copies of Transcripts

Colleges require that transcripts be sent directly from one institution to the other in order to verify accuracy of the information.

Official transcripts—transcripts sent directly from one college to another with the official seal of the institution.

Unofficial transcripts—working copies of your records that do not have the official seal stamped on the document and are often used to help students determine plans during the initial phases of the admission process. The unofficial transcript is also known as a worksheet.

Students can obtain instructions for transcript requests on the school's Web site or call the registrar's office. The instructions vary, but generally a request must include dates of attendance, former names (e.g., if taken a different married name), address(es) where copies should be sent, and social security number or student identification number. Transcript fees are low in cost—generally less than $10—and must be included with the request. A transcript request can be typed, but the registrar's office will need a signature in ink in order to release the information. Carefully following the instructions to request transcripts will help avoid delays.

What Is Accreditation and How Does It Affect Transfer Agreements?

"Accreditation" is a term used to reflect the status granted to an educational institution that has met or exceeded certain criteria. It is a rigorous "seal of approval" used by colleges to ensure the quality of an institution or degree program. Transfer of credit from one college to another is often dependent upon accreditation standards. The standard applies to the accreditation that the college held at the time that a student attended. For U.S. schools, accreditation is recognized by the Council for Higher Education Accreditation (CHEA), which has six regional accrediting bodies (see Appendix 3 on U.S. and international accrediting bodies). The regional nature of accreditation helps facilitate the transfer of credits from one institution to another.

There are other accrediting bodies, such as the Distance Education and Training Council (DETC); however, DETC accreditations are not as widely accepted as the regional accreditation. Colleges may review local programs and develop internal agreements called articulation agreements or seamless transfer agreements that state how the credits will be accepted. The general rule is that accredited colleges are more likely to accept credit from other similarly accredited colleges. Likewise, non-accredited colleges are more likely to accept credit from other non-accredited colleges. Even if a college is not regionally accredited, it may have high standards and offer excellent instruction. Accreditation may be an issue if students are considering transferring courses or doing graduate work.

How Much College Credit Will Transfer to My New Program?

Accreditation does not automatically guarantee the acceptance of transfer credit. The amount of credit transferred depends on many factors such as the college's transfer policies, type of degree, major, number of credits earned, and age of the credit (see Box 5.2). Some fields and subject matters such as nursing require that the learning be relatively current, so the age of the credit may be a factor.

Transfer credit rules are complex, so students must work closely with the academic advisor at the college who makes the official determination.

BOX 5.2   Transfer Credit

Students are more likely to receive transfer credits for credit that is:

- "C minus" or better grades. Rarely, colleges allow a limited number of "D" grades. Credit not completed or that received a failing grade will not transfer.
- 100 level or higher (college level). Credit for upper-division courses is transferred as upper-division (normally, 300–400 level) credit.
- in areas needed to complete the degree or certificate.
- not duplicated.
- considered academic level . . . technical or specialized coursework may be transferred only as electives, or it may be restricted or denied.
- acquired from a regionally accredited college.

Note: Credit that is earned in quarter hours, if needed, will be converted to semester hours.

Commonly, students who are denied transfer credit because the college they attended did not meet accreditation standards use the portfolio method to earn credit.

What Is a Diploma Mill or an Accreditation Mill?

"Diploma mill" is a term used to represent "dubious providers of educational offerings or operations that offer certificates and degrees that are considered bogus" (Council for Higher Education Accreditation Fact Sheet #6, May 2003). Students may also encounter accreditation mills which are "dubious providers of accreditation and quality assurance or operations that offer a certification of quality that is considered bogus" (ibid.). Both terms represent quick fixes, or an easy way to obtain a degree with little concern about mastery of knowledge, skills, or abilities. Council for Higher Education Accreditation (CHEA) provides a list of questions to help individuals identify diploma or accreditation mills (see http://www.chea.org/pdf/fact_sheet_6_diploma_mills.pdf).

How Do I Obtain International Transcripts?

United States colleges welcome international students to their campuses and distance education programs, but the transcript evaluation may take longer to complete. Some colleges complete their own evaluation of transcripts from foreign countries using published guidelines from such sources as the Council on International Educational Exchange. Most colleges require students to have their transcripts evaluated by a private organization because of the difficulty involved in assessing the titles, grades, and course levels. Students should select the agency recommended by the college they plan to attend and expect to pay about $100–$200 for the service. Once the credential evaluation is received from the private organization, a college will make its own decision regarding transfer credit.

Can I Appeal a Transcript Decision?

Colleges have guidelines for appeals if a student thinks that the decision made regarding transferability or placement of a specific course should be reconsidered. Sometimes supplying additional information such as course descriptions, letters from other colleges that have accepted the credit, or course syllabi can be useful for appealing a decision. However, students should understand that standardized rules are set by colleges so that every student's credit is assessed fairly, and there may be valid reasons for not transferring credit. Students may want to find out how the decision was made before going through a time-consuming appeals process. In cases where transfer credit is denied due to failure to meet accreditation standards, prior learning assessment can be the best option to gain credit when a student's learning is college level.

How Do I Obtain Transcripts for Military Service and Training?

The American Council on Education (ACE) has evaluated military occupations and training courses for academic credit since 1945. Credit recommendations are published in the *ACE Guide to the Evaluation of Educational Experiences in the Armed Services* (a reference tool used by college administrators). Military training, education, courses, and occupational specialty can be evaluated for college credit. For instance, according to ACE, the average number of academic credits awarded from an Army AARTS transcript is 14 semester hours (ACE Web site, 2005).

Students should start by obtaining their military records (Military DD-214) or training record (DD295 forms). If a copy of the discharge paper is unavailable, students can request one from the branch of the military in which they served. The ACE Military Program evaluates courses provided through the Air Force, Army, Coast Guard, Department of Defense, Navy, and the Marines. Credit recommendations for military occupations are based on the skills, competencies, and knowledge gained. ACE has simplified the process of assigning course recommendations by providing transcripts of military records and education. The ACE Web site provides a searchable course and occupation list.

After obtaining transcripts, if the record is incomplete, students should make requests for changes directly to the branch of the military in which they served. When a college receives the necessary official documentation, it will make the final credit determinations. Refer to Appendix 4 for specific information about how to obtain military transcripts.

How Do I Find Information on ACE Recommendations for Training, Certifications, and Professional Examination?

The American Council on Education (ACE), a private organization, offers a college credit recommendation service that has evaluated training courses sponsored by professional and nonprofit organizations, labor unions, Fortune 500 corporations, the government, the military, hospitals, businesses, and industry. In addition to evaluating training and certifications, ACE provides college credit recommendations for passing professional examinations. ACE conducts assessments by evaluating content, textbooks, level of instructions, classroom procedures, and expertise of the instructors. Credit recommendations are published in ACE National Guide to Educational Credit for Training Programs, a reference guide used by college administrators. The ACE Web site (http:///www.acenet.edu/nationalguide/) provides a searchable list of the training, certifications, and examinations that have been evaluated. Students who find that the training certification or exam they've passed has been evaluated can follow the directions on the Web site to download a request for an official ACE transcript.

What Types of Training Does ACE Recommend?

Box 5.3 shows a brief sampling of the training suppliers, credentials, and exams certified by ACE. Students should check the site frequently to see if ACE has added any new examinations or suppliers of training.

Does a College Always Follow the ACE Recommendations for Credit?

No, ACE only makes credit recommendations. The recommendations state the academic level such as vocational, lower division, upper division, or graduate as well as recommended semester hours.

Once ACE makes a recommendation, colleges have three options:

1. Accept the ACE recommendations
2. Not accept ACE credit
3. Accept the ACE credit but change the credit recommendations

BOX 5.3   Sample ACE Suppliers and Certifications

TRAINING SUPPLIERS EVALUATED (MORE LISTED ON ACE WEB SITE)	CERTIFICATIONS AND EXAMS (MORE LISTED ON ACE WEB SITE)
AT&T	The Association for Legal
Learning Tree International	Professionals
Lucent Technologies, Inc.	Certified Computer Programmer
Montessori Associates	Certified Novell Administrator
Mortgage Bankers Association	Certified Professional Secretary
of America	Certified Purchasing Manager
New Horizons Computer Learning	Chartered Financial Consultant
Centers, Inc.	FAA Pilot, Engineer, Mechanic
PADI International, Inc.	Licenses
Program National Inst. for	Microsoft Office Specialist
Automotive Service Excellence	Respiratory Therapy Technician
U.S. Postal Service	
Verizon Communications	

(See ACE guide for college credit for workforce training at: http://www.acenet.edu/nationalguide/)

What If My Training, Certification, or Exam Has Not Been Reviewed by ACE?

In addition to ACE-approved credit designations, some colleges accept national or state licenses such as real estate licenses, aviation licenses, and professional health certifications. Some colleges have investigated training programs and developed articulation agreements that detail how credits will be recognized at their school. If the program has not been evaluated by the college, students may have the option to petition for credit by writing a formal request with attached documentation. Even if the training is ACE certified, the college may ask for a more detailed explanation to make a credit determination. On page 62 is a sample petition for credit based on training. However, students should always follow the requirements of the institution they are attending.

If My Training or Certifications Are Not Evaluated, What other Methods Can I Use to Earn Credit?

Training records and certificates make excellent supporting documentation for building a portfolio for credit (see Chapter 11 on supporting documen-

BOX 5.4   Sample Training Evaluation Request

Petition for credit based on training, certification, or examinations

Contact information (name, address, phone number, e-mail, student identification number)

Type of degree seeking: Attach copies of planned coursework (degree plan) and official or unofficial copies of transcripts, if available.

Describe each training experience and the learning that you acquired from the training. Attach supporting documentation such as certificates, human resource records, course description, outline of the content, letter of verification, or instructor qualifications.

Title of training: Sponsoring institution that provided the instruction. Dates and hours of training.

Is the training or exam ACE recommended? (Yes or no.) If yes, attach a copy of the ACE recommendation.

Pre-training experience and preparation: List relevant knowledge and skills that you acquired before the training (include dates and names of organizations where you gained the knowledge, skills, and abilities). Describe any preparation you did before attending the training.

Training and learning: Describe the specific knowledge, skills, and abilities that you gained from the course. If used, describe or show the results of the evaluation method. Attach records or documents that verify the level of training and learning.

Post-training application of the learning: Describe how and where you applied what you learned. Describe the level of learning that you acquired.

Verification clause and signature:
I attest that the information provided and documents are a true and accurate description of training that I have received.

Signed _____   Dated _____

tation). Or, a student may use his or her knowledge to take a CLEP or challenge exam (see Chapter 6 on examinations).

Adult Learner Profiles

In our adult learner profiles, we met Andrew, who earned credit from a Bible college, and Tim, who earned credit through a technical college. Even though they could not transfer these credits directly (due to accreditation standards), both students were able to successfully petition for credit through the portfolio method.

Tim was able to receive one credit for a Microsoft 2002 Office Specialist Certification because the college he attended accepted the ACE-reviewed recommendations. Tim used the ACE Web site (www.acenet.edu) to obtain a transcript. While applying for her day care license, Maria obtained her CPR and first aid certification through the American Red Cross. Maria used her skills to assist children with minor injuries and to aid a child who fell off of a swing set and was seriously hurt. She used the training request form to obtain one credit in first aid toward her degree program (see Adult Learner Profiles, page 17).

REVIEW

1. Requests for official copies of transcripts should be sent as early as possible in the admissions process.

2. ACE provides college credit recommendations for accredited training, certifications, and exams as well as military service and education.

3. Colleges have the final decision about how many credits transferred are accepted and how they are applied.

NEXT STEPS

1. Review the list of learning created in Appendix 2: Prior Learning Inventory. Request transcripts based on your previous college, training, or military service.

2. Consider what prior learning assessment methods (such as testing or portfolio) could be used to demonstrate areas of knowledge and learning that are not accepted through transcript or training evaluation.

REFERENCES

ACE. (2005). Find an ACE-Reviewed Training Course Provider. Retrieved September 1, 2005, http://www.acenet.edu/AM/Template.cfm?Section=Organizational_Services&Template=/CMHTMLDisplay.cfm&ContentID=6034.

Council on Higher Education Accreditation (May 2003). Fact sheet on Diploma and Accreditation Mills. Retrieved September 1, 2005, http://www.chea.org/pdf/fact_sheet_6_diploma_mills.pdf.

ADDITIONAL RESOURCES

Web sites:

www.acenet.edu/nationalguide/
ACE National Guide to College Credit for Workforce Training

www.militaryguides.acenet.edu/
ACE Military Guide

www.chea.org
Council on Higher Education Accreditation (CHEA)
(Lists the United States Regional Accreditation Associations)

www.collegedegreeguide.com
This site provides an article about understanding accreditation. See: http://www.collegedegreeguide.com/articles-fr/accredited-college-university.htm.

www.degree.net
This site provides information on colleges and universities from the publishers of *Bear's Guide*.

Books:

Bear, J. (2003). *Bears' Guide to Earning Degrees by Distance Learning.* Berkeley, CA: Ten Speed Press.

The Bears' guides utilize the Generally Accepted Accrediting Principles (GAAP) to determine which schools are accredited. The Web site offers a more detailed explanation of the accrediting process as well as information on non-U.S. accrediting bodies.

Johnson, J., Robinson, L., & Welch, S. (2004). *Pocket Guide to College Credits and Degrees: Valuable Information for Adult Learners.* Washington, D.C.: American Council on Education.

This ACE guide answers many questions that adult students have about linking their career goals to college degree decisions, lifelong learning, institutional degree and credit transfer programs, distance-learning programs, and accreditation issues.

CHAPTER 6

Credit by Examination

What Some Students Have Said about Earning College Credit by Examination

"Test-taking was a great way to fulfill credits while I was traveling extensively for my job. I was able to earn 18 credits in three months' time."

—JOE, AN ADULT LEARNER

"I never thought I was a good test-taker, but after taking and passing seven CLEP and DANTES exams for a total 21 credits, I'm sold!"

—SUSAN, AN ADULT LEARNER

"I took a challenge exam (at the college) to waive the lower level course requirement for my computer science degree. I didn't study and passed with a 97 percent score. Passing the exam allowed me to enroll in the next level of programming courses."

—COREY, AN ADULT LEARNER

What Are the Advantages of Using Credit by Examination?

Earning credit by exam is a high-yield and low-risk option for students who have knowledge in such areas as mathematics, humanities, foreign languages, business, science, and history. Test-taking has several advantages. It is a convenient option for busy working adults who want to earn credits for learning or make up for missed courses. Test-taking is an inexpensive option because many standardized exams cost less than $100 for the equivalent of a three-credit course, which leaves students with more money to pay for coursework.

In addition, testing may be an advantage over the portfolio method for students who find it difficult to provide evidence to verify their learning. Students do risk losing the exam fees if they fail the exam, but failing a standardized national exam does not penalize a student's grade point average. However, failing a college-specific course challenge may have heavier consequences. Overall, for many adult students who have the learning, the benefits of test-taking outweigh the risks.

What Exams Will the College Accept?

As with other assessment methods, there are no ironclad rules. Each college sets policies on the type of tests and credit recommendations they allow.

What Types of Exams Are Available?

There are generally two categories of exams: college-specific challenges and standardized national exams.

College-specific course challenges

Course challenges, also known as exams for waiver or challenge exams, are offered by some colleges. Normally these exams are written and scored by the college's instructors and are based on the final for the course. Students should consult the testing center or an academic advisor for more information about challenge exams.

Standardized national exams

Standardized national exams are intended to test general knowledge in areas such as history, languages, art, science, and English, which are subjects required for most two- and four-year degrees. Standardized exams are written by professional testing companies or private universities and are administered in licensed testing sites throughout the country. The most common standardized tests that measure experiential learning are College Level Exam Program (CLEP) and Dantes Subject Standardized Tests (DSST), which was originally designed for the military (see Box 6.1). Additionally, some colleges—such as Thomas Edison, Excelsior College, and Ohio University—allow students outside their university to take the exams they have created. Finally, there are specialized tests such as the Test of English as a Foreign Language (TOEFL), which measures English language ability, and tests for nursing students offered by the National League of Nursing (NLN). See Additional Resources at the end of this chapter for Web sites and information on each of these exams.

BOX 6.1   Sample CLEP and DSST Exam Titles

CLEP Exam Titles	DSST Exam Titles
Humanities	**Humanities**
American Literature	Ethics in America
Analyzing and Interpreting Literature	Introduction to World Religions
English Composition	Principles of Public Speaking
English Literature	Technical Writing
Freshman College Composition	**History and Social Science**
Humanities	Art of the Western World
Foreign Languages	Western Europe since 1945
French Language (Levels 1 and 2)	An Introduction to the Modern Middle East
German Language (Levels 1 and 2)	Human/Cultural Geography
Spanish Language (Levels 1 and 2)	Rise and Fall of the Soviet Union
American Government	A History of the Vietnam War
Human Growth and Development	The Civil War and Reconstruction
Introduction to Educational Psychology	Foundations of Education
Principles of Macroeconomics	Lifespan Developmental Psychology
Principles of Microeconomics	General Anthropology
Introductory Psychology	Drug and Alcohol Abuse
Introductory Sociology	Introduction to Law Enforcement
Social Sciences and History	Criminal Justice
U.S. History I: Early Colonization to 1877	Fundamentals of Counseling
U.S. History II: 1865 to the Present	**Science and Mathematics**
Western Civilization I: Ancient Near East to 1648	Astronomy
Western Civilization II: 1648 to the Present	Here's to Your Health
	Environment and Humanity: The Race to Save the Planet
Science and Mathematics	Fundamentals of College Algebra
Calculus	Physical Geology
College Algebra	Principles of Physical Science I
Trigonometry	Principles of Statistics
College Mathematics	**Business**
Biology	Principles of Finance
Chemistry	Principles of Financial Accounting
Natural Sciences	Human Resource Management
Business	Organizational Behavior
Information Systems and Computer Applications	Principles of Supervision
	Business Law II
Principles of Management	Introduction to Computing
Principles of Accounting	Introduction to Business
Introductory Business Law	Money and Banking
Principles of Marketing	Personal Finance
	Management Information Systems
	Business Mathematics

(Source: CLEP http://www.collegeboard.com
DSST http://www.getcollegecredit.com/)

How Do National Standardized Exams and College-Specific Challenge Exams Compare?

Box 6.2 is a chart that compares two of the most commonly used national standardized examinations (CLEP and DSST) and college-specific course challenges.

What Are Some Types of Challenge Exams Offered by Colleges?

1. **Final exams or comprehensive exams** can be multiple choice, short answer, essay, or a combination, and may be based on lecture content and textbooks used for a specific course. Reading lists and course syllabi may be useful for studying (see Box 6.3).

2. **Demonstrations** are specific skills that are critical for competence (for example, a clinical nursing competency or a mechanical skill). The evaluator may give background on the demonstration beforehand so that the student can understand the context before completing the demonstration.

3. **Simulations** are used to replicate the conditions that a student might encounter. Computer simulations may be used if creating the actual situation would take too much time or set-up. For example, a student might demonstrate competencies in a range of computer software skills by taking a computer-generated competency test. Or an electronics department may have a computer-aided circuit simulation.

4. **Case studies** are types of tests the evaluator can use that allow a student to apply a skill set to specific circumstances. For example, students might be given a case study that describes a company's marketing challenges and would then be asked to analyze the problem and present a solution. Students may be allowed time to complete a project, such as to design a marketing campaign based on the case study.

5. **Interviews or oral presentations** with one evaluator or a panel may be required alone or in combination with an exam or portfolio. Interviews are opportunities for students to address specifics about their prior learning (see Box 8.5 on portfolio interview preparation). Or a student may be asked to prepare an oral presentation to challenge a speech requirement.

BOX 6.2 Comparison of National and College-Specific Exams

	NATIONAL STANDARDIZED EXAMS	COLLEGE-SPECIFIC COURSE CHALLENGES
Web sites	CLEP http://www.college board.com DSST http://www.get collegecredit.com	See the individual college's Web site.
Description	Exams written by national companies that are tested and normed by experts.	Exams written by instructors or obtained by the college to determine student competencies based on a school's course offerings.
Scoring and credit assignment	Score recommendations are published; however, each college determines whether to follow the recommendations.	The college determines the acceptable grade and credit assignment. In some cases, course challenges are used to waive a required course.
Type	Primarily multiple choice. A few exams require a written essay or fill-in. CLEP language exams have an oral portion where students listen to a tape.	Varies (see Box 6.3). Exam may require a take-home portion. An interview with a faculty member may be required.
Cost	Nonrefundable. Less than $100 for three-credit-hour exams.	Nonrefundable. Cost varies.
Timed	CLEP—90 minutes (Exception "English Composition with Essay"). DSST—not timed.	Timed or untimed, depending on the exam.
Where offered	Authorized testing centers throughout country. See Web sites for information.	Offered only at the college in a testing center or computer lab.
Retake policy	Students can retake the exams after six months.	Normally, no retake allowed.
Study guides	CLEP—published guidelines. DSST—fact sheets with guidelines on Web site (see Additional Resources at the end of this chapter).	Study guides offered at the college.

(continued)

	NATIONAL STANDARDIZED EXAMS	COLLEGE-SPECIFIC COURSE CHALLENGES
Impact on grade point average	None.	May affect grade point average. See individual college's policies.
Transcript	Title of course and number of credits earned appears on transcript.	Title of course and number of credits earned appear on transcript.
	Credit may appear as credit by exam or transfer credit (distinguished from course credit).	May or may not be distinguished as credit by exam on the transcript.

BOX 6.3   Preparing for College-Specific Challenge Exams

1. Students should find out as much information as possible about the competency they will be asked to demonstrate as well as the setting and evaluation tools used. When guidelines are provided, students should review them several times and follow the requirements with attention to detail.
2. Students should try to replicate the demonstration, oral presentation, or simulation as closely as possible when preparing or practicing for the actual exam.
3. In some cases, students can preview the type of simulation equipment that is used, preview an exam question, or visit the room where the test is conducted. Visualizing the room in advance can help decrease testing anxiety. To ensure objectivity and fairness, students should not expect an in-depth conversation about the exam with the evaluator.

What Steps Are Involved in Earning Credit by Examination?

1. Check the policies regarding credit by examination at the college or nearest test site before taking any exam. Policy statements may be in a catalogue, student handbook, or Web site under a heading such as testing, CLEP, credit by exam, advanced standing, advanced placement, adult learning or prior learning assessment. Students who are close to graduating should check the deadline for accepting credit by examination.

2. Double-check that the exam is acceptable for the credit needed. Unfortunately, students have jumped ahead and taken a test before verifying if the credit is acceptable, resulting in a loss of both time and money. Never assume, for instance, that a test will satisfy a foundational course in the major. It is easy to be deceived by looking at the title alone, but many factors go into the assessment of whether a standardized exam is the equivalent of a course, including subject, lower or upper division, and a student's course record. As this book has stated frequently, always verify the selections.

3. Select the exam that best matches the learning. Some students have the option of selecting one of several options (such as exams that will satisfy humanities credit). The best way to determine which exam is most suitable is to take several practice tests and select the one with the best results. "Don't test out of something that is totally foreign to you," says Mary Martin, testing assistant director (personal communication, May 20, 2005). The exams test both general knowledge and the application of that knowledge to different contexts.

4. Schedule the exam date at a testing center. Find a testing center at the college or find the closest testing center. Lists of authorized test centers that administer CLEP and DSST exams are published on their Web sites (see Additional Resources below). If currently serving in the military in the U.S. or overseas, there is the option of taking DSST tests on military bases. Students might schedule a time to visit the testing center to determine parking availability before their test day or arrange to view a sample CLEP test question on the computer screen and get more familiar with the forward and back buttons.

5. Obtain results. Generally, results are mailed to the student and the college that is indicated on the test score form. CLEP results are scored on the computer and available immediately, although official documentation may take a week or more. The required score for earning the credit varies from exam to exam, so students should check the college's minimum passing score for the exam.

What Information Can I Obtain from the Testing Center?

Testing centers have information on scheduling, fees, and registration. It is best to schedule a test at least several weeks in advance to guarantee a spot. Since the CLEP test is administered on a computer, there may be a limit on seating depending on the number of terminals available. Fees may be charged for changing or canceling a test date. The staff at the testing center can answer questions regarding time limits, check-in, form of identification needed, when to expect results, and re-testing (if allowed). In addition, the testing center can provide information on handicapped accessibility and can make accommodations for those with a documented disability as set forth by the Americans with Disability Act (ADA).

What Are Some Effective Ways to Review for an Exam?

When preparing to take an exam, it is important to review both content and test-taking strategies. The goal is that, when a test-taker walks into the exam room, she or he is as well prepared as possible to receive a passing score.

1. Review the study guides carefully. Take more than one practice test, if available, and closely examine the results.

2. Check libraries for study guides and reference books. (When checking out guides from the library, be courteous of others and don't mark up the practice tests). CLEP and DSST exam guides provide lists of general reference books. Study guides for national exams do not list a specific book that a student can study to pass the exam since the exams are based on prior learning. On the other hand, college-specific challenge exams are based on the textbooks for the course, so reviewing the texts can be beneficial. Many colleges make available the course modules or course syllabi to help students determine the textbook used and topics covered.

3. Spend time studying areas of weakness. It is less productive to spend equal studying time on each part of the exam. A better strategy is to determine which areas are strengths and then focus on the weaknesses. According to Richard Koch (1998), a person can accomplish a majority of what he or she needs (up to 80 percent) with only a small amount of effort (perhaps as small as 20 percent). With this principle in mind, students should be wise about where to focus their efforts.

4. Study key words and concepts. Be prepared to apply knowledge, concepts, and theories to different situations and real-life issues.

What Are Some Test-Taking Strategies?

1. Use the first guess. Research has shown that a first guess is often the correct response.

2. Determine if there is no penalty for guessing, mark an answer for every question.

3. Practice handling key words such as "best," "least," "correctly," and "not."

4. Create questions and answers if there are no practice questions.

5. Set blocks of time to study between work and family schedules. Short periods are more productive for memorizing than long stretches.

6. Collect study material in a separate briefcase in order to study on breaks during the workday.

7. Seize the most alert times of the day for learning (e.g., early morning or late at night), even if it is only for a 10- to 20-minute period (see also Gross, 1999).

8. Remember with intention. Motivation to remember makes the mind receptive to learning.

9. Anchor the learning with ideas and experience previously learned.

10. Explore a combination of methods to make studying an active, not a passive, process.

What Strategies Can I Use to Study Based on My Learning Preference?

Learning styles are preferences or approaches that describe how a person learns best. Most learners have a combination of learning style preferences, but one or two may be strongest. Students can use their learning style strengths or a mix of learning styles to keep the process of studying active. Box 6.4 lists strategies for studying that match visual, auditory, and kinesthetic preferences.

BOX 6.4   Test-Taking Strategies by Learning Style Preference

Visual learners: tend to learn through seeing or visualizing.
- study visual materials such as pictures, charts, maps, photos, and photographs
- use colors to highlight or underline key words (avoid over-highlighting)

(continued)

- visualize the concepts as pictures to assist memorization
- illustrate ideas as pictures
- create timelines for studying dates and add comment boxes
- use mind-mapping software or create mind maps with drawing tools
- write cartoons with bubbles to illustrate ideas
- use multimedia software such as PowerPoint to design a slide show
- watch videos on the topic
- study in a quiet place
- skim through reading material to get a rough idea what it is about before settling down to read it in detail (effective for all learning styles)
- create and publish a Web site of key terms and links to valuable resources

Auditory learners: tend to learn through listening

- talk to friends and family members about the subject area
- participate in community discussions on the topic such as a lecture on art history at a museum
- prepare a speech on the topic for a public speaking class or for a Toastmasters (public speaking) club
- read the practice questions and answers out loud
- use a tape recorder to record notes
- use some creativity to create a song, advertisement, jingle, or mnemonic device
- create and tell a story that demonstrates an application of the concept
- watch a video on the topic with another person and discuss the contents (see http://www.freeuniv.com)
- listen to audio tapes on the topic while driving and talk back to them
- brush up on a foreign language by listening to foreign language radio or television stations or hanging out in a store, coffee shop, or restaurant where the language is frequently spoken

Tactile or kinesthetic learners: tend to learn by doing something, moving, and touching

- walk or pace slowly while studying
- read while on stairmaster or exercise bike

(continued)

- squeeze a ball while reading
- use modeling clay to create a representation of a concept
- work standing up
- create flashcards in multiple colors and study the flashcards in groups of three
- set short blocks of time to study and then move around
- stretch muscles and move legs or arms while studying
- use the same music in the background during every study period
- find free Web sources and play simulations and games on the topic (www.merlot.org provides navigational links by subject matter and reviews free multimedia educational resources on the Web)
- purchase practice tests, if available, in an online or CD-ROM format (DSST program has an iStudySmart resource, which allows students to take in-depth study courses online, as written text, or in a CD-ROM format—see information in Additional Resources)

Is Test-Taking Anxiety Normal?

Absolutely. A level of test-taking nervousness is normal and very common. Many adult learners have been out of the classroom for a decade or more, so they may have less confidence in their test-taking ability. The anxiety may be due to any number of factors, including negative past experiences, a feeling of unpreparedness, or inexperience. Even though the anxiety may be uncomfortable, a small amount should not prevent students from trying this option. Students who feel paralyzed by test-taking anxiety may consider using the portfolio method to earn credit. There are a number of strategies that may be helpful for reducing testing anxiety, so conducting research on the Internet or in books or taking study skills courses can help such students find and experiment with stress-reduction methods. Certainly, adequate preparation is one of the best methods of reducing test-taking anxiety.

REVIEW

- Obtaining credit by examination can be a low-risk, low-cost, and high-yield way to earn college credit.

- Check the policies on credit by examination before registering and paying for an exam.
- Optimally, study both test-taking techniques and test content.
- Exams measure experiential learning, so students should choose tests that closely match their knowledge and experience.
- Maximize studying time by concentrating on areas of weakness and experimenting with a variety of active study techniques.
- Combining both testing and portfolio helps students earn credits in more areas than by using just one assessment method.

NEXT STEPS

1. Create a list of action items with a timeline for studying and taking an exam. Start with the exam date and fill in blocks of time to research, review, and take practice exams. Or use time-management software or a calendar to record the deadlines.

2. Navigate the CLEP (http://www.collegeboard.com) and DSST (http://www.getcollegecredit.com/) Web sites. What was the most useful information on the site? What surprised you?

3. Visit the testing center, if possible. Arrange for a quick tour of the facility. Prepare a list of questions before the visit and interview the testing staff.

4. Write or explain the pros and cons of using credit by exam for foundational courses.

5. Find useful Web sites or interview a student or students who have used the credit-by-exam method. What tips did they offer?

6. Determine the best study strategies based on experimentation.

7. Find resources on handling test anxiety and try one or two tips.

8. Research study materials such as books, videos, and audio recordings that will help in preparation for an exam. Many colleges and some local public libraries can assist students in borrowing material from other institutions.

REFERENCES

Gross, R. (1999). *Peak Learning: How to Create Your Own Lifelong Education Program for Personal Enlightenment and Professional Success.* NY: Putnam.

Koch, R. (1998). *The 80/20 Principle: The Secret of Achieving More with Less.* NY: Currency.

ADDITIONAL RESOURCES

CLEP (College Level Examination Program) testing

> Web site: http://www.collegeboard.com

> Study guide: CLEP Official Study Guide (current edition)

>> The guide has sample questions and answers for all 34 exams, information on getting credit for CLEP, and exam-taking tips. The guide also has a tutorial on CD-ROM to help you become familiar with the computer-based format of the exams.

>> Around 3,000 colleges and universities award credit for passing scores on CLEP exams. CLEP exams are divided into two categories: general examinations and subject examinations. CLEP exams penalize incorrect answers, so study the test-taking strategies. Most subject exams are the equivalent of three credits; a few are six or even 12 credits. The tests are offered on a computer and take approximately 90 minutes to complete.

DSST (formally known as DANTES Subject Standardized Tests)

> Web site: http://www.getcollegecredit.com/

> Study guide: Download individual study sheet for exams on the Web site. Available in PDF format.

>> There are over 37 test titles in the areas of social science, business, mathematics, applied technology, humanities, and physical science. Currently, there are around 1,700 colleges and universities that recognize the program and award college credit for passing scores. Approximately 37 tests cover business, physical science, humanities, social science, and applied technology. Most of the exams are multiple choice. There is no penalty for an incorrect guess on DSST exams, so test-takers should mark an answer for every question. Students on active duty in the military can go to a military base to take DSST exams free of charge. If the military base is inconvenient, active-duty personnel might be eligible for reduced rates at a college testing site.

>> The Web site iStudySmart.com offers in-depth study courses for DSST exams. These courses are available for a cost online, in CD-ROM format, or printed workbook format and are used in combination with college-level textbooks. Information on fees is available on the Web site. The Chauncey Group International has developed a comprehensive study guide covering the eight most popular business titles.

Education Testing Service

> Web site: http://www.ets.org

> Study guides: Study guides vary, and resource information is available online.

>> The Education Testing Service has information on the GRE exams, financial aid, and test-taking.

Nursing Challenge Exams

Web site: www.nln.org

Study guide: National League for Nursing Review Guide for RN Pre-Entrance Exam and National League for Nursing Review Guide for PN Pre-Entrance Exam

No penalty for guessing. There are three test sections consisting of multiple-choice questions, covering the following areas: verbal skills and reading comprehension, mathematics, and science.

Advanced Placement Examinations (A.P. Exam)

Web site: http://www.collegeboard.com

Study guide: A.P. exams are taken at the end of a year-long advanced-level high school course. These exams are developed through the College Board and administered by the Educational Testing Service.

Excelsior College Examination (ECE)
(Formerly Regents College Examinations ACT/PEP)

Web site: http://www.excelsior.edu/

Study guide: Information on study guides is available on the Web site.

Excelsior College Examinations meet specific college degree require-ments of the Excelsior College degrees and are accepted for college credit by over 900 colleges and universities. Offered by Excelsior College in New York, but other colleges may accept the exams. Exams are available in the liberal arts, business, and professional areas such as nursing and education.

Thomas Edison College Exam Program (TECEP)

Web site: www.tesc.edu/

Study guide: Information on study guides is available on the Web site.

TECEPs cover the humanities, social science/history, science and math, business, and professional areas such as counseling. Offered by Thomas Edison State in New Jersey, but other colleges may accept the exams.

Ohio University Exams

Web site: http://www.ohio.edu/independent.

Study Guide: Information on study guides is available on the Web site.

Course Credit by Exam offered by Ohio University, but other colleges may accept the exams.

Test of English as a Foreign Language (TOEFL)

Web site: http://www.ets.org/toefl/

Study Guide: Information on study guides is available on the Web site.

The TOEFL measures English language proficiency in reading, listening, and writing and is offered on computer in most regions of the world. In areas where access to computer-based testing is limited, a paper-and-pencil version of the test is administered.

Web sites on study skills:

http://sas.calpoly.edu/
Use the search tool on this site to find the Study Skills Library operated by California Polytechnic State University.

http://www.utexas.edu/index.php
Use the search tool on this site to locate the Study Tips section on the University of Texas site.

Book:

Ellis, D. (2006). *Becoming a Master Student.* Boston: Houghton Mifflin Company.

PART

III

Portfolio
Development

CHAPTER 7

Learning Theory and Application

"You do not really understand something unless you can explain it to your grandmother."

—ALBERT EINSTEIN

Why Study Learning Principles?

Prior learning assessment recognizes that experience alone, such as the number of years on a job, does not solely determine the awarding of college credit. Therefore, it is fitting to start this section with a review of learning definitions and principles. The process of unpacking learning is hard work because it requires recalling events. It also requires learners to carefully reflect on experiences and assess how the learning relates to college courses. As stated by Malcolm Knowles, "Performance assessment in the area of *understanding* and *insight* requires that a participant demonstrate his ability to size up situations, see patterns, develop categories, figure out cause-and-effect relationships, and in general, to apply knowledge and thought processes to the analysis and solution of problems" (1975, p. 87). Completing several exercises from the chapter will help students tap into the events that shaped their learning.

What Is Experiential Learning?

Learning can involve one or more methods, including memorization, study, classroom instruction, observation, and hands-on experience. Experiential learning, however, involves direct participation in, or observation of, an event. Learning occurs when participants gain something, such as an understanding, appreciation, ability, or skill. Thus, experiential learning involves direct participation or observation plus the acquisition of knowledge, skills, and abilities.

Notice the language (the strong nouns and verbs) Luckner and Nadler use to describe the experience of active learning:

What is experience? It is an event, training, activity, occurrence, adventure, experience, endeavor, lecture, outing, undertaking, project, seminar, quest, escapade, happening, or effort. The experience is nothing more than a reference point or marker in one's life. It can be overlooked, discounted, passed by, ignored, or forgotten. Then again, it can be the turning point, catalyst, energizer, enzyme, breakthrough, impetus, stimulus, incentive, or driving force for great changes and learning . . . What we bring into it, take from it, leave there, reach for, and continue to use, [is] all up to us. (Luckner & Nadler, 1997, xv)

Students who write about their experiential learning become more aware of future learning opportunities. In fact, they become mindful and purposeful about the learning experiences they encounter—they go looking for learning.

Learning occurs before, during, and after an event. Active learners approach situations by asking questions such as when, why, and how. In addition to learning how to learn and being more purposeful about learning, the process of writing and reflecting helps students become aware of the strengths and weaknesses in their learning style. After examining a business failure, one student stated, "If I ever start a business again, I will spend more time planning, researching, and finding the necessary amount of capital before I just jump in and launch my dream" (Smith, T., personal communication, October 3, 2004).

BOX 7.1 Experiential Learning

1. Describe one of the following:
   - a time where you learned a skill by trial and error
   - a skill you learned that you applied to a new situation
2. Write a step-by-step page of instructions on how to do something such as perform a computer function, play a sport, or operate a piece of equipment. What did you see, notice, observe, examine, watch, ponder, or think about when explaining your step-by-step process?
3. What are some ways you could become more deliberate about your learning?
4. What are the benefits of promoting a learning culture in an organization?

In What Ways Are Adult Learners Unique?

The study of adult learning gained momentum when Malcolm Knowles recognized that adult learners differ from their younger counterparts in a number of significant ways (1984). Knowles recognized that adults are self-directed learners. Secondly, Knowles and others have observed that adults approach learning as problem-solving and learn best when the topic is relevant to their life. As a result, prior learning experiences provide a rich basis for classroom discussion and learning. Adult learners personalize their learning—they apply the strategies and principles learned in the classroom at work. Teaching techniques such as case studies and applications have proven to be effective with adult learners. In accordance with these principles, instructors adopt the role of facilitator of students' learning rather than a lecturer or "sage on the stage."

BOX 7.2   Thinking about Learning

1. An adult learner with 20 years of experience on the job and a traditional-aged college student are both attending a course on organizational communication. Draw some inferences about the difference in learning styles between the two students.
2. Describe a time when you faced a problem in a work or volunteer setting. What information did you use to analyze the pattern? Did you propose a solution?

What Are the Strengths and Challenges of Experiential Learning?

Experiential learning (learning from experience) and traditional classroom learning differ. Certainly, learning in the traditional classroom environment has many advantages. Classroom learning benefits from an instructor who is dedicated to completing objectives to help students learn the skills, theories, and concepts needed in a field. In addition, for hands-on learners, classroom environments are like laboratories where learning is practiced, and students benefit from the input of other learners.

There are some drawbacks to classroom learning. Many students cram for exams and forget the knowledge they've gained because it is not applicable to their experience. Also, while many students are familiar with the theories and ideas in a classroom, they may not be able to apply the concepts to real-life settings.

One strength of experiential learning is that students acquire their knowledge in the field, with the assistance of experts and by direct application. One of the drawbacks of experiential learning is that it is very difficult to measure. In fact, there may be gaps in the learning. Students who learned primarily experientially are also generally less aware of the theories, principles, and concepts that underlie their learning, and therefore, are less transferable.

The main difference between the two ways of learning (experiential and classroom) has been described as input vs. outcome (Coleman, 1976, pp. 49–61; Whitaker, 1989, p. 2). Since the sources of learning differ significantly, the learning processes and outcomes, although similar, look and feel different. For experiential learners, the process of learning is through observation and doing (input) and the result is more inductive (outcome). That is, adults will observe and act in a number of situations and draw conclusions based on their participation. In classroom learning, a more deductive process occurs in which students study the conclusions from experts in the field in the classroom (input) and then apply the concepts and theories to specific instances such as case studies (Coleman, 1976).

When the comparison to classroom learning is applied to the assessment of prior learning, it becomes clearer why students who petition for credit based on experience may need to update their knowledge of the concepts that underlie their subject matter in order to make their learning more complete. Students may learn concepts reading books, talking with others, or training. According to Whitaker, when preparing the petition for credit, it is essential to leaven the mix of theory and practical application with ample portions of reflection. "The learning is not complete until the learner has some understanding of what both the theory and the practical experience mean. It isn't enough to have both in isolation; the learner needs to know why they are necessary [and] how each extends the value of the other" (1989, p. 14). Experiential learning benefits from the study of principles because they help students understand how their learning fits into a larger context.

What Is Tacit Knowledge, and How Does It Relate to Prior Learning?

Tacit knowledge is knowledge that we are largely unaware we are using—it can be a hunch, gut feeling, or response that thoughtfully draws from a

BOX 7.3   Linking Theoretical and Practical Experience

Survey the textbook that is required for a specific college course. Find several key concepts, terms, or theoretical models taught in the course. Key terms are often typed in a **bold-faced** font, and theoretical models are often illustrated in a graphic. If the course utilizes hands-on learning, locate several general rules of thumb that govern the subject matter. Or, navigate the tip database at http://tip.psychology.org. The site links to explanations of theories, learning domains, and learning concepts.

a. What theories or concepts did you find that closely match your practical experience or observations?
b. Does understanding the theory and concepts help extend the value of your practical experience? In what way?

large pool of knowledge (see Boud, Keogh, Walker, 1985, Kikoski & Kikoski, 2004). From *The Inquiring Organization*, "It is possible that each one of us knows more than we can say, that each individual possesses a vast reservoir of personal knowledge—that is yet 'unsaid.' The 'unsaid' includes the entire background of one's experiences, unarticulated assumption[s], and unconscious thoughts, as well as inferences drawn from them . . . What is 'unsaid' and 'unexpressed' could be the reservoirs of tacit knowledge. Tacit knowledge is the less familiar, unconventional form of knowledge . . . It is the knowledge of which we are not conscious, the knowledge that we cannot say. Tacit knowledge is the knowledge of which we are unaware, and unaware of using" (Kikoski & Kikoski, 2004, p. 66).

This tacit knowledge, or rich source of untapped knowledge, can be accessed by reflecting on events. Further, reflecting on experiences is an ". . . active process of exploration and discovery which often leads to very unexpected outcomes" (Boud, Keogh, Walker, 1985 p. 7). The process of understanding past events and assimilating new information stimulates the brain's reflective muscle. The brain makes connections with information, especially when it is personally relevant. Drawing on tacit knowledge leads to new understanding and, thus, to new learning.

The prior learning assessment process involves recalling past events. When students are involved in this level of reflection, new learning occurs.

BOX 7.4   Drawing from Tacit Knowledge

You have just been promoted to a supervisory or management position in your company. Drawing on your knowledge of organizations, describe two or three specific ways you could motivate your employees. Did the discovery of answers lead to insights that you had not previously considered?

What Are Intelligences, and How Do They Affect Experiential Learning and PLA?

Howard Gardner describes how multiple intelligences can work concurrently in the learning process (1983, 2000). Most people have several strong areas of intelligence. When students uncover their prior learning, they often recognize threads in their abilities and preferred learning styles. The intelligences include:

Logical-mathematical intelligence—consists of the ability to detect patterns, reason deductively, and think logically. This intelligence is most often associated with scientific and mathematical thinking.

Linguistic intelligence—involves having a mastery of language. This intelligence includes the ability to effectively manipulate language to express oneself with words or to remember information.

Spatial intelligence—gives one the ability to create and manipulate mental images in order to solve problems.

Musical intelligence—encompasses the capability to recognize and compose musical pitches, tones, and rhythms.

Body-kinesthetic intelligence—is the ability to use one's mental abilities to coordinate one's own bodily movements.

Interpersonal intelligence—allows one to understand the feelings and intentions of others.

Intrapersonal intelligence ("intra" means inside a person)—is the ability to understand one's own feelings and motivations.

Naturalistic intelligence—is the ability to discern and see subtle patterns in nature.

Spiritual/existential intelligence—is the ability to ponder questions about life, death, and ultimate realities. This intelligence is associated with the recognition of the spiritual.

In his work *Emotional I.Q.* (1995), Daniel Goleman recognized that high emotional I.Q. gives workers a competitive edge. Competencies in such areas as intrapersonal and interpersonal intelligence are often unrecognized, yet knowledge of self and the ability to work with others often leads to success in the workplace. Some of the personal and social competencies included in emotional I.Q. are self-awareness, self-motivation, persistence, empathy, and social skills.

BOX 7.5   Multiple Intelligences and Emotional I.Q.

1. Describe a process or a skill that you had to learn in order to succeed in your job. What intelligences did you most rely on the most? Least? For instance, a student who solved a telecommunication problem could use interpersonal intelligence to ask someone knowledgeable for help, linguistic intelligence to follow the verbal step-by-step instructions, and logical-mathematical intelligence to think through a program error.
2. Describe a workplace problem where you used intrapersonal and interpersonal intelligence to arrive at a solution.

What Does David Kolb's Cycle of Learning Include?

In his book *Experiential Learning* (1984), David Kolb described learning as a four-part cycle: concrete experience, reflection and observation, abstract conceptualization, and active experimentation. When each stage of the cycle is utilized, the learning is more complete; likewise, when a portion is left out, the learning is short-changed.

Kolb's model points to the often-neglected part of learning: careful observation and reflection. Kolb has developed a learning style inventory to help learners understand their preferences (see References). The cycle of learning shows how concrete experiences can lead to personal reflection on the experience. Next, the reflection can lead to conclusions or rules of thumb that derive from the experience, or the application of theories or concepts (abstract conceptualization). Finally, the conclusions reached lead to new ways of testing the learning (active experimentation), leading back to the next concrete experience (see Box 7.6).

The following descriptions and questions are adapted from Kolb's model of experiential learning. By targeting each quadrant, students can more effectively describe their learning around the cycle.

BOX 7.6   Kolb Model of Experiential Learning

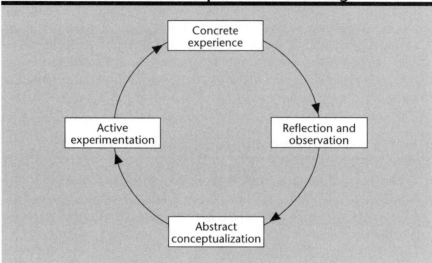

Concrete experience—Describe your experience. What did you do? What actions did you take? Common verbs: worked, created, prepared, implemented, conducted, produced

Reflective observation—What did you notice and observe about the experience? Common verbs: observed, watched, noticed, saw, thought, discovered

BOX 7.7   Using the Kolb Model

Ask a partner to question you about your learning in an area you plan to petition for credit. The questions should target each stage of the cycle. They should include:

- What did you do? (concrete experience)
- What did you notice? (observations and reflections)
- What did you conclude as a result of what happened? (abstract conceptualization)
- How did you apply your learning to future situations? (active experimentation)

Consider having your partner record your responses. This is a good warm-up activity for writing the experiential learning narrative, especially for oral learners.

Abstract conceptualization—What rules, theories, and concepts apply to this situation? Common verbs: concluded, theorized, found, realized, deduced, learned

Active experimentation—What happened as a result of your experience, reflection, and learning? How did you apply your learning to future situations? Common verbs: used, updated, applied, tried, implemented, changed

How Can Critical Incidents Demonstrate My Learning?

To demonstrate learning in their portfolio, students can give short accounts of critical incidents or events that had an impact on their learning. A critical incident is an event that resulted in changed thinking, attitudes, or actions. Those incidents, when described in detail, provide powerful testimonies of a student's learning.

Faced with such challenging problems as handling an irate customer, loading a computer, coping with project scope creep, or keeping a meeting on task, learners receive valuable insight on what to do differently in the future. Reflection on critical incidents provides opportunities for learners to gain feedback and learn retroactively (see Brookfield, 1990, Cooper, 1998).

BOX 7.8 Reflection on Critical Incidents

Critical incidents, when combined with feedback and reflection, provide learning opportunities. Use this three-step process to analyze a critical incident:

1. Describe a critical incident and your role in the incident. What happened? What did you do? How did you react?
2. Analyze the critical incident. In what way did this incident change you? What did you learn from this incident?
3. Describe how this incident influenced your future decision-making or behavior. How did future experiences help you more completely understand this incident?

 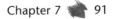

Reflection-in-Action

Donald Schöen states that when faced with complex problems, students and professionals are most successful when they practice the skill of reflection-in-action. Reflection-in-action refers to the ability to think about what they are doing *while* they are doing it (1987). Schöen believes that effective education includes coaching in the artistry of reflection-in-action (1987, p. xii).

How Can Bloom's Taxonomy Be Used in Critical Thinking and Reflection?

One of the most well-known educational models is Bloom's Taxonomy—specifically, the cognitive domain that emphasizes intellectual outcomes. The domain breaks down learning into cognitive levels, with the higher levels involving critical thinking (Bloom & Krathwohl, 1956).

Most college-level curriculum requires a level of critical thinking that is built on a foundation of basic knowledge and understanding. When analyzing a particular course, it is useful to estimate where the majority of the outcomes fit. For instance, some lower-level college courses emphasize knowledge and comprehension, while upper-level courses may require a higher level of application, analysis, and evaluation. It follows that, if a prior learning assessment candidate needs to demonstrate learning at the appropriate level, Bloom's Taxonomy can assist the student in using the proper terms.

BOX 7.9 Adaptation of Bloom's Taxonomy for PLA Students

LEVEL	DESCRIPTION	KEY WORDS/DESCRIPTION
Knowledge	What you can recall and describe such as facts, terms, and basic concepts.	What, where, when, which, how. Can you describe, define, recall, name, and explain your knowledge?
Understanding	Describing, clarifying, and explaining the concepts, facts, or ideas.	Demonstrate, compare, interpret, clarify. Can you explain your knowledge in your own words?
Application	Demonstrating how the concepts, facts, or ideas can be used.	Apply, experiment, do. How did you apply your knowledge to a specific situation?

(continued)

Level	Description	Key words/description
Analysis	Examine in more detail your decisions and actions.	Explain, categorize, deduct, problem-solve, ask why. Why did you arrive at your conclusions about the subject matter?
Evaluation	Judge the validity of the decision or action taken.	Evaluate, judge, make recommendations. What recommendations do you have as a result of evaluating your learning?
Innovation	Create or change something based on your previous learning.	Plan, change, create, innovate. What innovation resulted in your learning?

BOX 7.10   Levels of Critical Thinking

Review a course description and, if available, course outcomes or objectives from a course that closely aligns with your learning. What is your best estimate of the percentage of each stage of Bloom's Taxonomy that best matches this course? For instance, a business software applications course may draw 40 percent from the levels of knowledge and understanding and 60 percent from application. In contrast, a course in management strategies may draw more equally from all the levels, especially if the student applies the knowledge in critical evaluation of his or her work style (indicating high levels of evaluation and innovation).

BOX 7.11   Apply Learning Concepts

Using the learning concepts from this chapter, such as the Kolb model, read the following descriptions and decide whether you think the student's learning was:

a. complete
b. somewhat complete
c. incomplete

(continued)

Andrew

1. As a minister who has been called to difficult circumstances such as car accidents and the scene of a suicide, Andrew learned about death and dying. Andrew's knowledge of death and dying concepts come from his understanding of the Bible.
2. Andrew has read extensively on communication theory and has learned communication concepts from college textbooks. He's applied his understanding of the concepts to numerous experiences involved in television, radio, and ministry.

Tim

1. Currently, Tim is employed as a software developer, where he uses UNIX on a daily basis. Some of the commands he uses less frequently, but he knows that if he reviewed the commands, he would learn them quickly.
2. Tim was assigned to lead several large projects and managed them effectively. His understanding of leadership principles is limited to his IT experience.

Maria

1. Maria learned first aide and CPR (for adults and children) when she applied for her at-home day care licensure. While employed at Head Start, Maria used her first aid skills to assist children.
2. Maria works as a teacher's aide in a Head Start program. She attended several literacy conferences and workshops and has assisted the lead teacher in the classroom; however, she has not designed curriculum or lesson plans.

REVIEW

- Learning is an active reflective process that draws upon experience.
- Experiential learning (learning from experience), when compared to classroom learning, has both advantages and drawbacks.
- Applying related theoretical concepts and ideas to a practical experience helps students make their learning more complete.
- Tacit knowledge, often retrieved through reflection and analysis, leads to new learning.

- Many learning experiences use a variety of intelligences.
- The Kolb model of experiential learning includes concrete experience, reflection and observation, abstract conceptualization, and active experimentation. When students use the Kolb model to describe their experiential learning, they can target their writing to each stage of the process.
- Examining and reflecting on critical incidents assists the learning process.
- The higher levels of critical thinking, as demonstrated in Bloom's Taxonomy, are often required for learning at the college level.

NEXT STEPS

1. Review several exercises in this chapter to begin the process of thinking about your learning.
2. Conduct research on learning theories and concepts and find those that have application to prior learning assessment.
3. Spend some time every day for one week writing about your learning.

REFERENCES

Boud, D., Keogh, R. & Walker, D. (1985). What is reflection in learning? In D. Boud, R. Keogh, and D. Walker, (Eds.), *Reflection: Turning Experience Into Learning* (pp. 7–17). London: Croom Helm.

Bloom, B. & Krathwohl, D. (1956). *Taxonomy of Educational Objectives: The Classification of Educational Goals. Handbook I: Cognitive Domain.* New York: Longmans, Green.

Brookfield, S. (1990). *Using Critical Incidents to Explore Learners' Assumptions, in Fostering Critical Reflection in Adulthood.* Edited by J. Mezirow, pp. 177–193. San Francisco: Jossey-Bass.

Coleman, J.S. in Keeton, M. et. al. (1976). *Experiential Learning: Rationale, Characteristics and Assessment.* San Francisco: Jossey-Bass.

Cooper, D. (1998). *Reading, Writing and Reflection.* San Francisco: Jossey-Bass.

Gardner, H. (1983). *Frames of Mind.* New York: Basic Books Inc.

Gardner, H. (2000). *Intelligence Reframed: Multiple Intelligences for the 21st Century.* New York: Basic Books.

Goleman, D. (1995). *Emotional Intelligence: Why It Can Matter More Than IQ.* New York: Bantam Books.

Kikoski, C.K. & Kikoski, J.F. (2004). *The Inquiring Organization: Tacit Knowledge, Conversation, and Knowledge Creation: Skills for 21st-Century Organization.* Wesport: Praeger.

Kolb, D. 1984. *Experiential Learning: Experience as the Source of Learning and Development.* Englewood Cliffs: Prentice Hall.

Knowles, M.S. (1984). *The Adult Learner: A Neglected Species (3rd Ed.).* Houston: Gulf Publishing.

Knowles, M.S. (1975). *Self-Directed Learning: A Guide for Learners and Teachers.* New York: Association Press.

Luckner, J.L. & Nadler, R.S. (1997). *Processing the Experience: Strategies to Enhance and Generalize Learning.* Dubuque, IA: Kendall/Hunt.

Schöen, D.A. (1987). *Educating the Reflective Practitioner: Toward a New Design for Teaching and Learning in the Professions.* 1st ed. San Francisco, CA: Jossey-Bass.

Whitaker, U. (1989). *Assessing Learning: Standards, Principles, & Procedures.* Chicago: CAEL.

ADDITIONAL RESOURCES

http://www.hayresourcesdirect.haygroup.com/
Kolb, A. Learning Style Inventory. Published by McBer and Company. Learning style assessment based on the Kolb model.

http://www.barbsbooks.com/logic.htm
Quick Flip Questions for Critical Thinking based on Bloom's Taxonomy and developed by Linda G. Barton.

CHAPTER 8

Portfolio Contents, Assessment, Planning, and Learning Chronology

"After spending years raising our children, I was nervous about entering college. Writing the portfolio helped build my writing confidence and gave me a jump-start when I started my more challenging courses."

—MARIA, AN ADULT LEARNER

Why Create a Prior Learning Assessment Portfolio?

Previous chapters dealt with the procedures for earning credit for training (transcripts, military, corporate training, certifications) or through test-taking (CLEP, DANTES, challenge exams). Portfolio-assisted assessment was created to help assess the types of college-level learning that are not measured by other methods.

In Preparing the Portfolio, What Type of Assistance Is Available?

Due to the complexity of preparing a portfolio, many colleges offer non-credit workshops or credit-bearing prior learning assessment courses. Assistance may range from a meeting with an advisor to a three-credit course.

What Are Some of the Typical Contents of the Prior Learning Assessment Portfolio?

Depending on the college, contents of the portfolio may include some, or all, of the components listed in Box 8.1:

BOX 8.1 Typical Portfolio Contents

CONTENTS	DESCRIPTION
Title page	Title, name, identification number, contact information, and date.
Table of contents	Lists the contents of the portfolio.
Goal statements (or forms) Signature of authenticity	1. Statement of student's educational goal. 2. Statement on how prior learning assessment relates to educational goal. 3. Statement on courses or outcomes being petitioned for credit. 4. Statement of authenticity and signature. *Note: Some colleges have students notarize the statement of authenticity.*
Learning chronology	Resumé, learning chart, or learning autobiography with experience in chronological order.
Prior learning narrative or competency statements (repeated for each subject or outcome being petitioned)	Extensive learning narrative or competency statements matching the student's learning to the college-level course or outcomes being petitioned.
Index of supporting documentation	Lists of supporting documentation that verifies the learning.
Supporting documentation	Supporting documentation, numbered with captions.
Transcript copies and degree plan	Working copies of degree plan and transcripts to verify that credit being petitioned meets requirements for the student's goal and is not duplicated by previously earned credit.
Evaluation forms	Form used by evaluator to write the credit recommendation.

What Is a Prior Learning Narrative, and How Does It Differ from a College Research Paper?

The prior learning narrative is a narrative that demonstrates a student's learning and describes a variety of lessons learned based on the subject matter being petitioned. The narrative is not a term paper or research paper, although definition or theories from books may be woven into the narrative. The narrative is written in first person, using "I" (e.g., I concluded, I revised). The writer uses specific stories, examples, and details to describe learning on the subject matter.

The prior learning narrative may also be known as:

- Prior learning essay
- Experiential learning essay
- Portfolio narrative
- Competency statements
- Learning narrative

What Are Competency Statements?

Competency statements are sentences that identify what a student knows, what a student can do (skills and abilities), and the level of achievement. In programs such as education or health care, competency statements may be used in lieu of the prior learning narrative. An example of a competency statement: "I know and can use the principles of classroom techniques, both verbal and nonverbal, to encourage students to stay on task."

Why Spend Time Planning the Portfolio?

For busy adults, carefully planning the portfolio avoids wasted time and effort. One student recommended reading the entire contents of the portfolio manual or Web site that the college offers, not just scanning the contents. Then keep a checklist of items that need to be completed and meet the deadlines.

What Are the General Guidelines Evaluators Use for Awarding Credit?

Students should determine the specific criteria the college uses for assessment. Some colleges use the course outcomes or competencies; others use more general standards to determine college-level learning.

The following are general guidelines based on the CAEL standards. Colleges may set additional criteria (see CAEL standards in Chapter 4).

1. The learning narrative and supporting documentation demonstrate the student's learning as related to the criteria set by the college.
2. The learning demonstrates college-level achievement.

 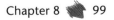

3. The learning demonstrated is considered at 70 percent ("C minus" grade) or higher.
4. The learning demonstrates an appropriate level of conceptual or theoretical knowledge as well as application, depending on the subject matter being petitioned.
5. The learning demonstrated is transferable to other contexts.
6. The credits awarded are lined up to fulfill requirements toward a student's degree or goal.
7. The learning for which credit is being petitioned cannot be duplicated by previously earned credit.

How Is the Portfolio Evaluated?

Generally, the portfolio is evaluated on a pass or no pass basis (see evaluation options in Box 8.2). In this case, if the portfolio does not pass, the

BOX 8.2   Portfolio Assessment Evaluation Options

Award full credit
Evaluators can award the full amount of credit petitioned by the student.

Award partial credit
Evaluators can award partial credit. Some programs do not allow the evaluator to split credit (e.g., give one credit instead of three).

Award more credit than requested
Evaluators may determine that the petition is exceptional and award more credit than the amount a student petitioned.

Deny credit
Evaluators can deny credit.

Request an addendum or interview
Evaluators may request additional information or an interview before making a final credit determination. In such cases, it is advised that the student follow the evaluator's request thoroughly and quickly because a deadline may be imposed. After the addendum material is submitted with the original portfolio or an interview is completed, the evaluator has the option of either awarding or denying the credit.

student's grade point average is not affected. A few colleges require evaluators to assign a grade to the portfolio. The evaluator determines the number and type of credits awarded and provides a written explanation for the decision. After assessment, students receive a copy of the credit award and a written explanation of the evaluator's rationale for the credit decision, and the credit is posted to the student's transcript.

If the Credit Is Denied, Can I Get My Money Back?

No. The assessment fees are paid upfront regardless of whether credit is awarded.

What If I Disagree with the Evaluator's Assessment?

Most schools have a policy for appeals so that a student who is denied credit can request to have the portfolio re-assessed. However, at most colleges, appeals are rare. After reviewing an appeal, the evaluator can ask for an addendum, award full or partial credit, or deny the appeal. A second appeal is not allowed.

What Steps Will I Take to Prepare and Submit the Portfolio?

BOX 8.3   Portfolio Project Steps

PROJECT STEPS	DESCRIPTION	DATE
One: Discover	Discover sources of learning. Prepare a preliminarily list of the courses that best match the learning and the degree plan. Request letters of verification and begin gathering supporting documentation.	
Two: Write	Draft and write prior learning narratives or competency statements.	
Three: Organize and edit	Organize supporting documentation and compile portfolio contents. Determine final credit petition. Edit writing.	
Four: Submit	Submit portfolio and pay the assessment fee to appropriate office.	

(continued)

Project Steps	Description	Date
Five: Receive notification	Receive formal notification by letter on credit determination.	
Six: Credit recorded	Credit awarded is transcipted (recorded officially) by the college's registrar.	

How Many Pages Should the Portfolio Be?

The length of the portfolio depends largely on the number of credits being petitioned and the complexity of the subject matter. Students should edit the portfolio and select supporting documentation to avoid redundancy. A well-prepared portfolio, including forms, narratives, and supporting documentation, may be 15 pages or longer.

How Long Will It Take Me to Create a Portfolio?

Some students take a prior learning assessment course and finish the portfolio by the end of the course. Other programs offer extensions or allow students to continue to petition for credits throughout their program. The portfolio must be assessed in time to allow the credits to be transcipted before a student's graduation.

How Do I Select the Course (or Outcomes) and Number of Credits to Petition?

Determining the courses or outcomes to petition is a process of discovery that is refined throughout the entire portfolio process (see Box 8.4). Ultimately, the evaluator determines the final credit award, but the student targets the areas he or she thinks the evaluator will use to determine credit.

Some students overestimate the amount of credit they could realistically receive; others underestimate the amount. One student stated, "The best advice I have is to work closely with an advisor. Initially, I thought I'd petition for six elective credits based on my paralegal work, but my advisor encouraged me to petition for nine credits based on three legal courses. I was glad I followed her advice" (Reed, T., personal communication, October 1, 2004).

BOX 8.4 Process of Selecting Credits to Petition

1. Consult your learning databank (see Appendix 1). Initially, brainstorm as many potential sources of learning as possible.
2. Compare your learning to the outcomes for a college course by consulting course descriptions and outcomes. Eliminate sources of learning that would not be considered college level. For instance, one student planned a large wedding for over one year; even though she learned about negotiating, planning, and budgeting during her wedding preparation, she could not match the experience closely to the outcomes of a college course.
3. Refine your list of course petitions against your goals with the assistance of an advisor. Check for duplication of previously earned credit (see also Chapter 3 on PLA planning).
4. Revise the list, as needed, when you prepare your portfolio. The portfolio process may help you uncover areas of learning that you did not previously consider.

What If My Learning Doesn't Fit Very Neatly into a Category?

Students whose learning doesn't fit neatly into a college course or competency will benefit from taking a prior learning assessment course or talking with a faculty member or advisor.

One student, who was interested in petitioning for credit after completing two tours in Vietnam, was advised to submit his entire body of work for assessment. After some revisions, the student was awarded 30 credits in a variety of subject areas, including global issues, photojournalism, radio broadcasting, screenwriting, and adult spiritual life and growth.

Another student's learning came from his 10 years as a recovering alcoholic. His commitments to Alcoholics Anonymous led him to open several AA chapters in local prisons. His learning didn't fit neatly into a category, but the college he attended awarded competency credits in areas such as motivation and leadership and alcohol addiction. Some colleges provide databases or lists of possible courses or competencies that can be used to petition for credit.

Can I Earn Credit for Travel Experiences? What about Significant Family Events?

It is possible but more difficult to earn credit for travel or family experience because college-level learning requires a level of understanding that typically does not occur with travel experiences as well as transferability of the learning to a broader context (see standards 2 and 3 in Chapter 4).

If an Interview Is Required, How Do I Prepare for It?

Students who are required to be interviewed by an evaluator should think positively about the opportunity to defend their lifelong learning. Students can prepare for the interview by finding out information about the requirements, including the type of questions, standards for evaluation, number of interviewees, location, and length (see Box 8.5). Interviews may be conducted by telephone or in person.

BOX 8.5   Portfolio Interview Preparation

Content: The following areas may be addressed in an interview:

1. Learning—How does the portfolio demonstrate your learning on the subject matter?
2. Transferability—Does the portfolio demonstrate that your learning is transferable to other contexts?
3. Relevance—Does the portfolio demonstrate that your learning is current (as appropriate to the field)?
4. Authenticity—Does the portfolio represent your original work?
5. Reliability and validity—Does the portfolio provide a reliable and valid demonstration of your learning?

Delivery (may be adapted if the interview is by telephone):

1. Arrive on time. Respect the time limits.
2. Know the contents of the portfolio to avoid shuffling through pages for answers.
3. Maintain eye contact.
4. Speak with appropriate volume and enthusiasm.
5. Ask for clarification on the question, if needed, before answering.
6. Monitor nervous gestures and avoid verbal fillers (e.g., um, you know).
7. Finish the interview confidently with a brief summation of the strengths of the portfolio.

What Is a Learning Chronology, and Why Include One in the Portfolio?

Preparing the learning chronology helps the learner recall and organize their learning experiences (see Box 8.6 and 8.7). As students prepare this part of the portfolio, they begin to reflect on their learning. The completed learning chronology helps the evaluator understand the context in which a student's learning took place. Depending on the college's requirements, students may include one of the following options as part of their portfolio:

- resumé or expanded resumé with or without training records
- chart that demonstrates what a student knows and can do
- narrative (learning autobiography)
- philosophy statement (e.g., philosophy of education)
- life history paper
- chronological record

A learning chronology provides students with an appreciation of the knowledge gained in a number of settings and the ability to see the threads in their learning. The process of writing a learning autobiography has numerous personal benefits as well. According to Terry Durkin, who made extensive use of the PLA process in Canada, "The big picture gets lost in the detail[s] of day-to-day living. Taking stock of my life was an intense emotional experience for me . . . the difficult things seem to give you the greatest sense of achievement" (1998, para. 4). Students often remark that seeing their accomplishments is a great motivator.

If I Include a Resumé in My Portfolio, What Format Should I Use?

Many students include a standard resumé in their portfolio. The resumé included in your portfolio can be easily tailored to the prior learning portfolio by including the knowledge, skills, competencies, and training gained in areas being petitioned for credit. Or, if a student has had relevant learning in a volunteer capacity, the experience can be added to a chronological or skills resumé.

What Are Some Warm-up Activities Used to Prepare the Learning Chronology?

BOX 8.6   Determining Roles and Responsibilities

Adult students juggle many roles and responsibilities. Write eight to ten different roles or responsibilities you currently juggle or have juggled in the past. These roles may help you identify areas of significant learning. Here's an example:

- Parent
- Student
- Spouse
- Son
- Front-line supervisor
- Union negotiator
- Home-budget manager
- Volunteer for Boy Scouts

Reflection questions on roles

- What roles do you juggle every day?
- What roles often collide or are in conflict?
- What roles provide the most satisfaction?
- What competencies do you demonstrate when you are in each role (see Appendix 2, part 3 for competency verbs).

BOX 8.7   Timeline

Drawing and labeling a timeline is an excellent prewriting activity to help students recall significant life events in chronological order. To create a timeline:

1. Draw a timeline horizontally across your page using paper or computer software. Starting with your high school graduation date, draw increments of five years. You might project five years into the future to indicate goals.
2. Plot significant events by the year on your timeline. You could include personal experiences, work, military service, and volunteer experiences.

(continued)

3. Draw branches off the significant events and add key words demonstrating the skills and knowledge acquired during that time period.

Reflection:
What were the major turning points in your life?

What events were dissatisfying at the time but proved to be valuable learning experiences?

What Does a Learning Chart Include?

The purpose of the learning chart is to help students explore their learning—the knowledge and abilities they've gained from experience. A learning chart can be formatted as a table and placed horizontally on a page. Below is an excerpt from one type of learning chart.

BOX 8.8   Learning Chart

SOURCE OF LEARNING: PLACES AND DATES	PRIMARY RESPONSIBILITIES (EXPERIENCE)	COMPETENCIES (AS RELATED TO POTENTIAL COURSE PETITIONS)
		• Knowledge • Abilities
Radio Station KCRS Public Relations 1990–95	Assist radio station in public relations and community building efforts.	Assist in preparation of public relations materials. Write, edit, and proofread public relations materials. Measure, reevaluate, and report efforts. Write fact sheets, news releases, and grants. Set up and implement publicity efforts such as trade shows, fairs, and fundraisers. Develop and maintain contacts with advertisers and community leaders. Utilize word processing software.

(continued)

SOURCE OF LEARNING: PLACES AND DATES	PRIMARY RESPONSIBILITIES (EXPERIENCE)	COMPETENCIES (AS RELATED TO POTENTIAL COURSE PETITIONS)
		Speak to community groups about the station. Work effectively with sales staff and diverse populations.

Continue chart with each major source of learning.

What Questions Will Help Me Write a Learning Autobiography?

When writing, students can incorporate the following questions.

BOX 8.9   Questions for Learning Autobiography

- Where did you learn what you know, what was your title, and what years did you serve in this position?
- Where and when did you decide to pursue your current goal? Who influenced you?
- Why was this experience significant?
- What did you learn at each stage that you didn't know before?
- How did the experiences you had change your beliefs?
- What deeply held values have come from cultural and gender experiences?
- What messages did you receive (or not receive) about the importance of a college education?
- What are some central ideas or philosophies that you have developed in regard to your field?
- If someone were to watch you perform, what knowledge, skills, and abilities would they witness? What personal qualities would they observe?
- What level of learning have you achieved?

BOX 8.10 Life Changes

Writing an autobiography is an opportunity to think about the changes you've experienced.

For example:

1. Changes in relationships and families.
2. Changes in the workplace.
3. Changes in your community.
4. Changes in your beliefs.

As you write, tune in to the metacognitive process, the process of knowing that occurs when monitoring one's own awareness and judgment.

What Are Some Guidelines for Adapting to the Audience (the Evaluator)?

1. Since the evaluator does not usually meet with the student in person, the learning autobiography serves as an introduction to that student.
2. The evaluator is particularly interested in understanding the context for learning that a student will petition.
3. The evaluator can award credit only for learning after high school, so the emphasis should be placed on learning after high school.
4. The autobiography will help the evaluator understand when there are gaps, such as when a student took time off to raise a child or start a business.
5. Evaluators are busy college instructors who appreciate a succinct narrative, so students should stick to the page-limit requirements. Although all learning is significant and important, spend less time discussing learning not considered college level (such as typing or balancing a cash drawer).
6. The learning autobiography does not need to reveal highly personal, sensitive information that is not relevant to the subject areas being petitioned. However, it is valuable to balance statements on skills and knowledge with reflection on life experiences. Communicating such areas as deeply held values, lessons learned, the impact of role models, and how culture or social status has shaped your life adds depth to the narrative.

What Types of Transitional Phrases Are Useful for Writing the Learning Autobiography?

To help the reader follow the chronology of events, students can use transitional words and phrases.

BOX 8.11   Examples of Transitional Phrases

Chronological:

- In 1995, I started the next phase of my career . . .
- During 2000–2004, I worked for . . .
- Summarizing the next five years (1995–2000) . . .
- In 2002, the business . . .
- By 2003, I was . . .
- In May of 1990, I took one of the biggest risks of my life . . .
- For the last 20 years, I have been employed with AT&T in numerous positions.

Topical:

- My skill set had grown tremendously, so I was ready for a new challenge.
- Even though my personal life took a downward turn, my spiritual life and volunteer activities during this time were gratifying.
- During the next six years, I received training from the police department in a number of areas, including...
- After experiencing a second downsizing in the organization where I worked, I looked more closely at my goals.
- During the next five years, I made up for my string of poor financial decisions.
- In the aftermath of hurricane Katrina, my family and I relocated.

How Can I Organize the Learning Autobiography?

The following excerpts demonstrate methods of organizing a learning autobiography.

Introduction: State learning from early years succinctly (move quickly to learning after high school).

My family moved from a small town in New Jersey, where I attended elementary school, to Southern California, which at the time seemed like moving to a foreign country. I grew up thinking that I'd follow in my father's and grandfather's footsteps and take over the family construction business. However, when the construction business took a downward turn, I entered the world of computers. Little did I know that I'd spend the majority of my adult life in the IT field.

Body: Include specifics on the context for the learning (when and where) and what was learned (knowledge, skills, and abilities).

In 2001, I was transferred to the newly formed customer support department and became a customer representative. My responsibilities included responding to all complaint calls and trouble-shooting problems related to the rollout of our services. At the same time I was learning UNIX and started to converse with the software engineers.

Specify the types of training received.

In 1987 when I started a day care, I completed CPR, first aid, and advanced CPR training through the American Red Cross.

After raising my children, I found that working as an early childhood educator was fulfilling because of the numerous training opportunities I received through the Head Start program. I also attended a conference in teaching in a multicultural classroom, which consisted of sessions on such topics as diversity, learning styles, and teaching manipulatives (mathematics).

Conclusion: Summarize the learning and state educational and career goals.

I made a promise to myself that I would complete a bachelor's degree before my sons finished college.

REVIEW

- Colleges use the portfolio method to assess the types of college-level learning that are not measured by other assessment methods.

- Evaluators can award full or partial credit, deny credit, or request an addendum.
- Spending time planning the portfolio saves students time and energy.
- Selecting the course or outcomes and number of credits for which to petition is a process of discovery that can be refined while preparing the portfolio with the assistance of an advisor.
- Students should follow the college's requirements for writing a learning chronology, autobiographical narrative, or resume.
- Preparing a learning chronology helps students recognize threads and patterns in their life and appreciate the learning that has resulted from experience.

NEXT STEPS

1. Review the portfolio-assessment procedures at your college.
2. Review the steps for completing your portfolio and create a checklist and timeline for completion.
3. Reflect on your life's events by completing a warm-up activity such as a timeline.
4. Use the learning chronology to refine your selection of areas to petition.
5. Receive feedback on your draft from an online writing lab (OWL) or an editor.

REFERENCE

Durkin, T. (July 1998). PLA in Search of the Diploma (Speech given at the 1998 PLA conference in Canada). Retrieved November 15, 2004, from http://www.tyendinaga.net/fnti/prior/plafn_tl.htm.

ADDITIONAL RESOURCES

Web sites:

http://owl.english.purdue.edu
   Purdue University's online writing lab (OWL).
http://fcis.oise.utoronto.ca/~plar/
   University of Toronto Web site on prior learning assessment and recognition (PLAR). Annotated list of publications.
http://www.tesc.edu/plasearch/
   Thomas Edison State College database of PLA course descriptions.

Books:

Mann, C. (1993). *Credit for Lifelong Learning.* 4th edition. Bloomington, IN: Tichenor.

Michelson, E., Mandell, A. & Contributors. (2004). *Portfolio Development and the Assessment of Prior Learning: Perspectives, Models, and Practices.* Sterling, VA: Stylus Publishing.

Parker, Y. (2002). *Damn Good Resume Guide.* Berkeley: Ten Speed Press.

Regis University Faculty. (2002). *Prior Learning Assessment: The Portfolio Process.* GA: XanEdu Publishing.

Thomas A. Edison State College. (1990). *Portfolio Assessment Handbook. 1990–91.* Trenton, NJ: Thomas A. Edison State College.

UMUC. (2002). *The EXCEL Course Guide.* Prior learning in cooperation with Office of Instructional Development, Undergraduate Programs. College Park: University of Maryland University College.

Vermont State Colleges. Office of External Programs. (1991). *Earning College Credit for Prior Experiential Learning: A Student Resource Packet for Educational Assessment and Portfolio Preparation.* Waterbury, VT: Vermont State Colleges, Office of External Programs.

CHAPTER 9

Research, Organization, and Prewriting Strategies

Why Is It Critical to Get Clarification from the College on the Format?

Although there are similarities, every college has different requirements for the format, style, and length of the written portion of the portfolio. Students should request clarification or view samples, if available, instead of submitting a portfolio that misses the mark. Some colleges prefer a formal written narrative; others prefer competency statements or charts that demonstrate the learning.

Why Research and Organize my Thoughts First?

Students have described writing the portfolio narrative or competency statements as a challenging but rewarding task. Research saves students time and energy. It is not a good idea to sit down and start writing a diary of random thoughts and stories related to their learning. Research helps students stay on track by targeting the course topics, key words, key theories, concepts, or skills to be covered. Also, conducting research helps students determine and describe their level of achievement.

What Course Research Is Useful to Conduct?

Since colleges frequently revise courses and outcomes, students should seek the most up-to-date information available (see Box 9.1).

BOX 9.1 Course Research

Type of Research	Availability	Usefulness to Prior Learning Student
Course Description • States number of credits (semester or quarter hours) • Course number indicates lower or list key level • Describes course	Readily available on college's Web site or in a published bulletin.	Somewhat useful as a starting point. Determines college level. Determines credit award (semester or quarter). Description may list subject areas.
Course outcomes • Sentences that describe the learning results	May or may not be available on a syllabus, on a Web site, or from the academic department. Provides topic areas.	Very useful. Helps students understand the expectations for a student who passed the course.
Course syllabus • Instructor-specific summary of topics and requirements	Less readily available. May be obtained from instructor or department.	Somewhat useful. May identify key content areas areas (see Box 9.2).
Course textbook(s) • Books required or recommended for the course.	Available in a college's bookstore. (Note: It is not always necessary to consult or buy the text.) A copy may be available in the college's library reserves.	Somewhat useful. Describes key theoretical principles or concepts. Helps student understand the depth and breadth of learning required. Highlights key terms and vocabulary associated with college-level subjects.
Subject matter-related textbooks, Web sites, or academic articles.	Available. Quality varies. Students should select highly academic, credible, and relevant sources.	Somewhat useful. May help remind students of key theoretical principles or concepts related to the subject matter.
Interview with Evaluator	May or may not be available. Evaluator may be available upfront to discuss general guidelines for the portfolio. Evaluator is generally unavailable for feedback during the writing process due to need for objectivity in assessment. (Students may obtain feedback on writing from a portfolio course instructor or advisor.)	Useful. Evaluator has expertise in subject matter and the level of learning. Evaluator may indicate preferences such as types of supporting documentation to include in the portfolio.

What Elements of a Course Syllabus Are Useful for Writing about My Prior Learning?

A course syllabus may provide some guidelines for students who want to petition for learning based on the course. Not all course syllabi have the same elements (see Box 9.2).

BOX 9.2 Syllabus Research

ELEMENTS OF SYLLABUS	PRIOR LEARNING ASSESSMENT
Course description	Identifies number of credits and level of course (lower level, upper level). The most useful course descriptions provide specific topic areas.
Course objectives or outcomes	Clear descriptions of the learning required as a result of taking the course. May indicate key principles or concepts covered.
Explanations of assignments	Identifies key areas, principles, or skills covered.
Course breakdown or breakdown of assignments	May pinpoint subject areas that are emphasized.
Requirements for the final exam or project	May help determine the level of achievement required.

What Is the Difference between Lower-Division (or Lower-Level) and Upper-Division (or Upper-Level) Coursework?

At most colleges, lower-division classes are numbered 100–299. Lower-division courses may be introductory, foundational, or survey courses. Community colleges do not offer upper-division classes. Upper-level courses, usually numbered 300–499, are more advanced courses that may have prerequisites (courses that must be completed first). Students usually take lower-division courses before enrolling in upper-division courses.

In the case of petitioning for prior learning credit, some colleges require that prerequisite or lower-division courses be fulfilled (through coursework or by portfolio) before a student petitions for upper-division credits. Additionally, the student should be aware that upper-division courses may require an advanced level of learning.

Can I Match My Learning with Course Descriptions from Other Accredited Colleges?

This will depend on the college's prior learning assessment policies. Some colleges allow students to petition for courses from accredited colleges other than the one they are attending (see Appendix 3 on accreditation). The stipulation is that the college the student is attending does not offer the course.

For instance, if a student has extensive background in intercultural communication, and the college does not offer the course, the student may be allowed to find a course description from an accredited college to use as a basis for awarding credit. In this case, the credit would be awarded at the institution where the student was enrolled and would be transcripted under a general category such as "communication, lower-division elective" (see Box 9.3).

BOX 9.3   Locating Accredited Colleges' Course Descriptions

To locate other colleges' course descriptions, students can use the Internet to search a specific college's Web site, such as:

1. Go to www.petersons.com. Conduct an "Education Search" by "Major."
2. Search for results by the subject matter or department (e.g., intercultural studies or communication).
3. Locate the college's Web site and navigate the site to find course descriptions. Or use a search engine using the following instructions:

   - Enter the subject matter. For instance, an "intercultural communication" course description may be found by entering "intercultural communication" + "course description" in the search box.
   - Scroll through the results and select sites with ".edu" in the Web address, indicating courses offered in educational institutions (avoid ".org" and ".com" sites).
   - Print the description, url, publication date, and name of the college for verification.

What If There Are Outcomes in the Course That I Don't Know?

Students who petition for full credit in a course (normally three credits) should be able to demonstrate their learning in the majority of the course outcomes. Sometimes studying a minor component will bring the student's knowledge up to par. If a student does not have learning in a significant area covered in the course, he or she should select another course to petition. Some institutions offer theory workshops to help students master this missing component of their learning.

Can I Adapt Course Outcomes to Reflect Experiential Learning?

Some colleges allow students to adapt course outcomes to better reflect the criteria for experiential learning (see sample below, provided by Donna Younger, personal communication, August 28, 2005).

The outcome on the syllabus for a course in business communication included a reference to a specific text that students were required to read. The fundamental knowledge reflected in the outcome addressed basic elements of negotiation and negotiation skills. In Box 9.4 below, the student rewrote the outcome to reflect the fundamental knowledge:

BOX 9.4   Revising Outcomes

OUTCOME FROM BUSINESS COMMUNICATION SYLLABUS	REVISED OUTCOMES
"Students will be able to articulate the four steps in negotiation from Simpson's *The Art of Negotiation* and describe how they might be used."	"Students will identify one model of negotiation, describe the negotiation process, and use it to critique a case study drawn from their work experience."

What Are Some Ways to Organize the Main Points of My Narrative?

The following are a few organizational strategies commonly used. However, students should use the organizational structure recommended by their college (see Box 9.5).

BOX 9.5   Organizational Strategies

The following are several methods commonly used to structure the narrative.

1. **Organizing the narrative using course descriptions:** Business Writing (the 3-credit course description as published in the 2000 Bulletin below).

   > BA202   Business Writing (3)   2000 Bulletin
   >
   > This course addresses business communications, including information requests and replies, letter forms, sales letters, memoranda, and report preparation.

   Structure: This narrative will demonstrate my writing competencies (knowledge and skills) gained from preparing:

   - information requests and replies
   - letters and memoranda
   - reports

2. **Organizing the narrative using key topics:** Management of Human Resources

   Structure: This narrative will demonstrate my learning related to the following human resources areas:

   - interviewing
   - employment offer
   - customer service
   - compensation and motivation
   - heath care and mental health benefits
   - relevant OSHA laws
   - training
   - ethical considerations

3. **Organizing the narrative using course outcomes:** Public Speaking

   Outcomes describe the results of the learning, or what a student who passed the class is expected to know. Students should address all of the major course outcomes, but may need to combine similar topics.

(continued)

Structure: The following discussion of my learning will follow each of the course outcomes, which include:

- Demonstrate the ability to recognize and select appropriate topics for oral presentations.
- Demonstrate the ability to logically organize and provide oral presentations.
- Demonstrate the ability to locate and cite sources of information.
- Demonstrate the ability to use effective verbal and nonverbal delivery techniques.
- Demonstrate the ability to adapt speeches to specific audiences.
- Demonstrate the ability to utilize technology to compile information and enhance oral communication.
- Evaluate speeches using listening, reasoning, and content-analysis skills.
- Incorporate critical thinking skills and argumentation principles into speech analysis and presentations.

4. **Organizing the narrative using a chronological approach:** Web Page Design

Students may also consider a chronological approach, but must be careful to address the course outcomes.

Structure: My experience related to designing Web pages is best described by using the following building blocks:

- understanding the client and server system and the Internet
- using html to create graphs and charts and to format pages
- using Web-authoring software to create animation and effects
- refining Web pages to be user-friendly
- creating a company intranet

How Do I Use a Prewriting Technique Such as a Mind Map?

Prewriting exercises such as mind maps help the writer put his or her thoughts to the page and avoid writing block. Mind maps are visual diagrams that help students visualize the structure and recall related details before writing. Students can draw the mind map, use a graphics program, or use the drawing toolbar to create their images on the computer.

Starting at the center of the page, write the name of the course in the middle, and then draw spokes that correspond to outcomes or topic areas. Next, draw small branches off the spokes and add words to describe related key words. This should be a brainstorming process, so the ideas should come quickly. Later students can develop a formal outline.

If I'm Required to Write a Narrative, What Is the Standard Organization and Format?

The standard structure for the narrative includes an introduction, body, and conclusion (see Box 9.6).

BOX 9.6   Standard Narrative Format

Introduction	Introduces topic, provides a unifying thesis, introduces the structure of the narrative. Main points covered in the narrative may be listed.
Body	Topics are divided topically or chronologically. Development and support of each topic. Some colleges require **bold-faced** headings.
Conclusion	Restatement of thesis and most meaningful points. Closing ideas.

What Are Some General and Specific Editing Tips?

In the final step of writing the narrative, students should thoroughly edit the contents because evaluators place high expectations on quality content when making credit determinations. Students are strongly suggested to use writing resources offered by the college, such as an OWL (online writing lab). Or students might ask a classmate, friend, or colleague for editing assistance.

General editing tips

1. Check that the content and illustrations match to the course.
2. Check for sufficient details to demonstrate learning.
3. Check for accuracy.
4. Check for grammatical and spelling errors.
5. Check the flow so that the illustrations easily unfold for the reader.

Specific editing tips

1. Don't rely on the spelling and grammar checker.

   Example: principal and principle are often used incorrectly
   Grammar checks may not catch the incorrect use of apostrophes.

   Example: The manager's (possessive when you mean plural) or it's (meaning "it is," when you mean possessive)

2. Avoid clichés or overused phrases.

   Examples:
   - It went without saying
   - Hit the nail on the head
   - My other half
   - Stuck out like a sore thumb
   - I was not the least bit concerned

3. Replace multiple words with one or two.

   Examples:
   In the near future (replace with "Soon")
   With the exception of (replace with "Except for")

4. Watch over-capitalization.
   Capitalize proper names of people, places, organization, institutions, and corporations.

   Examples:
   I served with John Brown in a volunteer capacity in Colorado.
   I was a customer service representative for SBC Communications, Inc.
   After high school, I transferred to Metro State College of Denver.

5. Check verb and pronoun consistency.

   a. Keep verb tense consistent. This can be difficult when shifting from an explanation of a past event to a present revelation. Most commonly, the narrative is written in past tense to reflect prior learning.

   b. Keep pronoun use consistent. Use first person (I/we) or second (you), but do not combine the two.

6. Use strong verbs.

   Example: I had an interview with a client. Replace "had" with "conducted" (cannot "prepare an interview")

7. Include the "actor" (subject) with the action verb.

   Before: Changes to the project lifecycle should always be communicated. (No actor stated)

   After: I remember one instance when I made adjustments to the project's lifecycle, but I failed to communicate the changes to the stakeholders. The results were disastrous.

What Is Plagiarism and What Steps Can I Take to Avoid Plagiarism?

Plagiarism is using someone else's written material or work as one's own. Colleges have adopted strict academic honesty policies partly in response to students who are able to easily cut and paste material from the Internet. In addition, many colleges subscribe to services such as www.turnitin.com, which is used to detect plagiarism in students' papers. To avoid plagiarism, students should locate a reference manual and use the style of documentation recommended (e.g., APA, MLA) and always use their original ideas. The general rule is, if in doubt, cite the work.

**Adult Learner Profile**

Maria divided her "Introduction to Communication" narrative into three sections—public speaking, interpersonal communication, and group communication—using the topical approach (see sample in Appendix 6).

REVIEW

- Students should make sure the portfolio builds the right contents and that the content matches a student's educational plan, learning, and the course objectives or outcomes.
- Conducting research on the requirements and criteria for evaluation helps the writer maintain focus.
- Using prewriting and editing strategies assists students in the writing process.

NEXT STEPS

1. Search for course descriptions or outcomes closely related to your learning.

2. Conduct research on the requirements for the learning narrative and the topic areas that you will address in the narrative.

3. Try a prewriting strategy such as a mind map to prepare the structure of the narrative and to brainstorm ideas.

4. Write an outline for the narrative based on the mind map or other brainstorming exercise.

REFERENCE

Younger, D., Colvin, J., Dewees, P., Graybill, M., & Michelson, A. (2005). *PLA 101: Prior Learning Assessment Workshop Manual.* Chicago: CAEL.

ADDITIONAL RESOURCES

www.apastyle.org/
> APA style tips and reference.

www.mla.org/
> MLA style tips and reference.

CHAPTER 10

Writing about Learning

After targeting, researching, and organizing the content of the narrative, students should aim to write the best possible explanation of their learning. In fact, the demonstration of the learning is the most critical ingredient in the portfolio. Some colleges require students to write competency statements that describe learning outcomes; others require a lengthy formal narrative. Either way, the challenge for the writer is to provide sufficient detail about the learning for the evaluator to make a credit decision. The task requires that the student describe what he or she learned about the subject matter with sufficient analysis to demonstrate college-level thinking.

In order to stimulate their recall of past events, students may consider talking with colleagues about their experiences. To stimulate analysis of key concepts covered in the targeted course, students might review textbooks or read current literature in the field. Due to the unique experiences and wisdom of the writer, no two learning descriptions are alike; in this way, writing the learning narrative is more art than science.

Students should avoid exaggerating their abilities or roles in projects; on the other hand, they shouldn't underplay the scope of their experience and learning. The evaluator is an expert in the field who may recognize if a student fabricates theories or manufactures evidence.

Even though the task is challenging, especially when writing within the confines of course outcomes, the results are rewarding. The road to learning is rarely linear. It is paved with unfortunate incidents and important insights, boredom and breakthroughs, mistakes and momentous events. The opportunity to capture and reflect on prior learning experiences yields new learning.

This chapter presents seven writing strategies for describing experiential learning, but there are certainly more writing strategies than this chapter describes. Depending on the college's requirements, implementing one or more of these writing strategies will assist students in describing their learning.

Seven strategies for writing about learning:

1. Write a detailed description that matches a learning outcome and incorporate key terms.
2. Describe and reflect on a critical incident.
3. Write the steps taken when learning a skill or ability.
4. Integrate definitions and concepts to demonstrate higher levels of learning.
5. Demonstrate problem-solving ability.
6. Write competency statements with strong action verbs.
7. Indicate the level of learning achieved.

Strategy 1: How Do I Write a Detailed Description of My Learning?

Tips:

- Use detailed examples to demonstrate the course outcome.
- Use terminology appropriately and in context.
- Describe knowledge, skills, and abilities.
- Refer to supporting documentation in the description (see Chapter 11).

The following excerpt demonstrates one learning outcome:

Public speaking: Demonstrate the ability to use effective delivery techniques (one of eight outcomes discussed in the narrative).

This excerpt lacks detail about the student's skills and abilities related to the topic of delivery.

Poorly written excerpt: public speaking

Every speech I gave for the United Way was an opportunity to use effective delivery techniques. I would arrive early and determine if I had a place to put my notes. I would survey where the audience would sit. There were several speeches where I used some pretty emotional details, which I thought [were] overdone. I watched other speakers who just read from their notes when the[y] presented, gave the facts, and didn't even stay for questions. I even saw a person fall asleep. I knew my presentation skills were better. I never wanted an audience member to fall asleep when I spoke.

The following excerpt provides sufficient details to demonstrate the student's delivery skills and abilities. Key terms are applied to the learning.

Improved excerpt: public speaking

> *When I gave speeches about my company for the United Way, I learned how to improve my delivery. I arrived early to every event to make sure that I had the set-up I needed. I preferred to use several flash cards with my notes so that I could keep my eyes on the audience. I remembered the lesson I learned from several years in Toastmasters. In Toastmasters, we were buzzed with a loud noise when we added fillers such as "uh." Those painful moments broke me of that annoying habit.*
>
> *Since I am only five feet tall, I avoided standing behind big podiums, allowing the audience to see my gestures and me to see their faces. When I was nervous, I had the tendency to use too many gestures, so I tried to tone them down. I am generally a loud speaker and never had a problem with volume or enunciation.*
>
> *One time I had a co-worker time my speech, and what I thought was a five-minute speech was only three minutes. I needed to slow down and add pauses, which took practice. I even wrote "slow down" in large letters on my note cards.*
>
> *Another aspect of delivery that was important in public speaking was appropriate dress. I always dressed professionally and more formally than casual business attire. I wanted to make sure that the audience took my message seriously. Finally, I didn't pace because there was often little room to move around, and I feared tripping on wires in high heels. I stood with my feet firmly planted and shoulder width apart. Paying attention to my delivery helped me keep the audience's attention and make a good impression. I received several accommodations for my efforts.*

Strategy 2: How Do I Write a Critical Incident to Demonstrate My Learning?

Tips (see critical incidents and Kolb model, Chapter 7):

- Describe an incident. Answer the questions who, what, where, why, when, and how.
- Add a reflection on the learning.
- Conclude with an application of the learning.

Excerpt: customer service and support:

As a technician in the air-conditioning service business, my service motto was "prevent disaster." In 1996, a large hotel in Las Vegas was planning to bring in a new piece of equipment to cool an exclusive part of the hotel. At my company, anything in Las Vegas that involved cooling a casino was top priority. I was working on the machine when I noticed a serious problem with one of the unit's large fans. I knew that if the machine wasn't running at the designated time, disaster was around the corner.

I sat down and analyzed every possible solution to resolve the problem. This situation occurred on the weekend, so I had no support from the office. Assessing the need for quick action, I made all the appropriate calls to have the manufacturers ship parts overnight. When the packages arrived at the hotel, I worked extensively over the weekend to install the parts and bring the machine online before the deadline. Through the entire ordeal, I learned that by using critical thinking and applying fast action, I could find a solution. Over the subsequent six years I've had in customer service positions, I have used my skills in critical thinking and have applied them to avoid countless other customer disasters (Brewer, J., personal communication, October 25, 2004).

Strategy 3: How Do I Describe Steps in My Learning?

Describing stages or instructions can be useful for demonstrating learning in areas such as creating a work of art, conducting legal research, programming a computer, or resolving an electrical circuit problem.

Tips:

- Demonstrate and describe learning progression from novice to expert.
- Personalize systematic instructions by adding colorful details and commentary. Identify and evaluate learning preferences. For instance, some students learn best from formal classroom instruction. Others learn by jumping in and making mistakes before consulting a manual or an expert.
- Summarize or condense the steps, if needed, to focus on advanced skill levels.

Sample competency in narrative format: "Ability to use HTML formatting codes to create basic Web pages"

Seven years ago, I completed a course on HTML (HyperText Markup Language) (see Document 4). Immediately, I had to use the < > buttons on the keyboard to create HTML opening and closing tags.

During this course, I learned how to create an HTML template on Windows Notepad (see sample 5a). I started every page with <html> and ended with the corresponding closing tag </html>. I learned that if I didn't put the closing tag, I could mess up my document in a hurry. I learned how to play with the commands. As shown in sample 5, I used the appropriate tags to add a title (<title>) in bold (<bold>). Some tags didn't require a closing tag such as <hr>, which is a horizontal line. I wrote the HTML code for a hyperlink ("href" stands for hypertext reference) <a href="URL"> Text Here to Activate Link</a> as in <a href="http://www.google.com">Link to Google</a>.

A similar pattern was used for creating e-mail links, as in: <a href="mailto:timk@att.com">Contact me.</a> When I viewed the results through the browser, I could check my work. It helped to keep the browser window open for this purpose. . . . Using my basic template, I could move to more advanced level where I created and formatted a table (Lee, T., personal communication, November 1, 2004).

Column competency statement format:

DESCRIPTION OF EXPERIENCE	LEARNING FROM EXPERIENCE	DOCUMENTATION
I know how to identify and use different HTML codes to format my documents.	I learned how to create opening and closing tags and view my results through a browser and make corrections. I learned how to properly format a header and footer.	Document 5—Course certificate in HTML from CompUSA (1995)
I can modify HTML documents using a text editor.	I learned formatting tags such as bold, underline, and italics. I learned HomeSite software.	Document 6—Sample of HTML using WordPad. Document 7—Sample using HomeSite Web-authoring tool
I can write Web pages that present information and graphics and provide hypertext links to other documents on the Internet.	I learned how to format tables, write hyperlinks, and insert graphics into my document.	Document 8—Sample 6 Shows hyperlink code Document 9—letter from employer

BOX 10.1 Writing Warm-up Activity

Characterize your learning using "from . . . to" statements.
See examples below:

From limitations . . . to unlimited.
From failure . . . to learning (then repeat the cycle).
From one way . . . to many ways.
From doing . . . to understanding.
From simplicity to complexity to simplicity.
From my window . . . to worldview.

Strategy 4: How Do I Integrate Knowledge of Concepts in My Writing?

Tips:

- Demonstrate understanding of the concept by applying the knowledge to an experience (see adaptation of Bloom's Taxonomy in Chapter 7).
- Cite relevant research. Include a reference page of sources.

Excerpt from methods of music/elementary education:

Fraction proportion, pattern, division, and other math concepts represent a few of the building blocks used in understanding music. Famous mathematicians such as Pythagoras (sixth century BC) first noted that the fractional pitch relationships in the lengths of strings have particular patterns in music (for example, half of a string makes the sound an octave higher). Another famous mathematician, Leonardo of Pisa (1200 BC), who was called Fibonacci, discovered a number pattern that works by adding two preceding numbers to find the third: 1, 1, 2, 3, 5, 8, 13, 21. The Fibonacci pattern has many applications to music, science, art, and literature. In music, the pentatonic scale has five notes (2+3); the diatonic scale has eight notes (3+5). The Fibonacci numbers that children enjoyed discovering are the octaves—the eight white keys and the five black keys on the keyboard. By recognizing Fibonacci numbers in my music class, students enhanced their music and math skills.

Furthermore, to distinguish a waltz from a march, I taught my students math in order to recognize the meter signatures involved. After learning the math concepts, the children could move or dance in threes (3/4 time) or march in fours (4/4 time). The lyrics of the songs also convey match concepts. A song and accompanying activity that my third graders enjoyed was "Frog in the Bucket," an American song (see document 5). When one out of the four children was inside the "bucket," the class would happily announce the fraction "1/4." Or, when two of four were in the "bucket," the student would say "2/4." . . . By analyzing the mathematical aspects of a song, the meter or time signatures, and the short and long sounds of the notes, I applied the standard knowledge of mathematics (Baxter, R., personal communication, February 9, 2005).

Excerpt using competency model: methods of music

DESCRIPTION OF COMPETENCY	LEARNING FROM EXPERIENCE	DOCUMENTATION
Identify and teach mathematical concepts as they are employed in music.	I know and can teach children to discover Fibonacci numbers: octaves, the eight white keys, and the five black keys on the keyboard.	Documents 3–5
	I know and can teach children to distinguish between a waltz and a march using movement and dance.	
	I know and can teach fractions using song and movement such as "Frog in the Bucket."	

Additional excerpts integrating concepts and experiences (from a variety of subject areas):

Write a lead-in to a definition.

One of the workshops I attended taught empathic listening skills, and we practiced the technique by dividing into pairs and trying role-plays. Empathic listening was defined by the speaker as . . .

List books or articles read. Include a reference page at the end of the narrative.

*During this period of re-organization, I read several books on managing change. Tom Peters writes, "Success will come to those who love chaos—constant change—not those who attempt to eliminate it" (*Thriving on Chaos*, 1987, p. 394). These books helped me understand that organizational stability was gone for good and I needed to adjust.*

Describe information gained from an interview.

I interviewed an owner of a salon, who gave me details about record-keeping methods and legal issues I might encounter. Also, I consulted an attorney who provided me with information such as . . .

Describe personal study.

From living in other countries and appreciating other cultures, I observed that Latin and Asian cultures seemed more concerned about establishing a personal relationship before getting down to business. I applied this understanding when . . .

Strategy 5: How Do I Write Competency Statements?

Some colleges ask students to write competency statements instead of a narrative. Below are tips for writing competency statements.

Tips:

- Describe knowledge, skills, and abilities used in a specific context.
- Identify actions that are observable and measurable.
  - □ Knowledge ("I know . . .")
  - □ Skills and ability ("I can do . . .")
  - □ Level of achievement ("At . . . level")
- Use strong verbs to describe learning. See lists below.

Knowledge and comprehension: classify, compare/contrast, conceptualize, define, describe, differentiate, explain, express, identify, illustrate, judge, know, label, list, name, paraphrase, practice, recall, review, select, state

Skill and ability: analyze, apply, assess, create, conceptualize, construct, create, demonstrate, design, develop, discuss, employ, examine, experiment, find, formulate, implement, invent, manage, plan, prepare, present, question, report, respond, solve, summarize, teach, use, write

Sample competency statements (from a variety of subject areas):

- *I implemented the fourth grade reading intervention goals and strategies to meet and exceed our individual literacy plan goals.*

- *I analyzed my golf swing on a videotape in order to improve my follow-through, lowering my average league score to 91.*
- *In order to accurately respond to client inquiries, I summarized and prepared bi-monthly reports on current regulatory and industry changes that affected clients.*
- *After completing two seminars on using Westlaw for searches, I learned techniques to locate case laws and experimented with terms and connectors and natural language to locate the maximum number of cases that were on point.*
- *As the assistant coordinator of public relations, I conceptualized and created a style guide for all grant writers in our organization in order to ensure a higher level of accuracy and consistency when applying for federal grants.*
- *I explained and applied the principles of ceramic processes such as glaze formulation, mold-making, and firing methods at a level of ability that allows me to teach an advanced ceramics course at a local art studio.*
- *I applied my understanding of the seven-stage mediation process to help resolve a labor dispute at my workplace.*
- *I gained knowledge and practice in installing hardware components such as hard drives, RAM, CD-ROMs, cables, and processors in my job as a technical services technician.*

Strategy 6: How Do I Demonstrate My Problem-Solving Abilities?

Tips:

- Demonstrate critical-thinking skills by analyzing a problem with sufficient detail.
- Describe and evaluate the solution.
- Describe the writer's role in the process.

Excerpt: Conclusion to the narrative on records management

Document management is such a critical part of our business operation, and I have learned so much since I established and implemented this program.

The support of my general manager was necessary to begin the process. If I did not have the support of my management team, this project would not have succeeded. In addition, I established a records-management team to assess our information system in order to identify the unmet needs and prioritize needed systems or improvements to our system. I wanted to establish a records-retention schedule that worked for our staff and find a user-friendly software program that would operate on our network and allow us to integrate electronic imaging.

The conference I attended and the listservs I consulted provided invaluable resources and answers to my questions. From this extensive process, I learned about communication and about my own skills and abilities. I confirmed to myself that my organizational skills and attention to detail allowed me to complete this project and establish an extremely effective company-wide system.

I received high praise from our management team, and the work that I did was reported to the board of directors. Our corporate attorney also praised my efforts; in fact, he told me that he has shared our information with many other corporate attorneys for use at the organizations they are representing. The culmination of this project was the presentation of the records management manual to our senior management team. This manual was used by all personnel and contained information on policies, procedures, and methods for our records management program.

Bottom line, it was satisfying to deliver a product that will be invaluable to my organization's future (Salazar-Ball, A., personal communication, January 20, 2005).

Strategy 7: How Do I Describe the Level of Learning I've Achieved?

There are several methods to describe a student's level of learning, as described below. Ultimately, however, the evaluator determines the level of learning achieved.

Tips:

- Compare level to the learning outcomes in a college course.

  I achieved a level of learning that is comparable to an introductory college photography course.

- Compare the level to another source such as ACE recommendations.

  My level of learning is comparable to the ACE guide recommendation for training in Microsoft Word, Excel, PowerPoint, and Access. (ACE recommends one hour each in computer applications or information technology in the lower-division category.)

- Compare the level of learning to an outcome (result of learning).

  I gained sufficient knowledge and experience to meet and exceed the learning described in the outcome—knowledge of literacy theories and practices.

- Compare level to other learners to a similar context.

  My experience in the preparation and interpretation of financial and operating reports for several small businesses is comparable to the knowledge and ability required of an entry-level accountant.

- Compare the level of learning needed to perform a specific job function.

  My ability is at a sufficient level to pass the examination and be employed as an on-call sign language interpreter for the state of California.

- Compare the current level of learning to an earlier level of achievement.

  I worked as a C++ programmer for two years before receiving a promotion as wireless software developer.

- Use supporting documentation to demonstrate the level of achievement or level of responsibility required for a position, such as:
  a. Coursework or training records
  b. Licenses or certifications
  c. Letters from employers or experts in the field
  d. Job descriptions
  e. Performance reviews

REVIEW

- There are many strategies for writing about learning. After researching and organizing their writing, students should follow their college's guidelines and write the best possible description of their learning.

- Students should not exaggerate or underestimate their ability, but write an accurate, well-supported, and complete demonstration of their learning.
- Using specific details, explanations of concepts, and strong competency statements helps build the student's credibility.

NEXT STEPS

1. Using your research and outline as a guide, write a narrative or competency statement to describe your learning.
2. Review the narrative or competency statements several times to add sufficient details to demonstrate learning at the college level.
3. Edit your writing. Use an editing service, if available.

CHAPTER 11

Compiling Supporting Documentation and Submitting the Portfolio

Note: The references to supporting documents used in this chapter are samples. The actual supporting document is not included in this book.

What Is Supporting Documentation?

Supporting documentation is also known as documentation, artifacts, or exhibits. These items demonstrate or verify a student's learning. Categories of documentation (Whitaker, 1989, p. 56) include:

a. Verification of accomplishment—articles, meeting minutes, programs, reports, customer surveys, prizes
b. Testimony regarding competence—performance evaluations, letters of verification, accommodation letters
c. Learning products—work samples, art objects, computer codes, written work or publications, Web sites, contracts, lesson plans
d. Certifications—evidence of licenses, training records, ranks
e. Other direct evidence—test scores, videos of performance
f. Descriptions—job descriptions, membership requirements, syllabi

Whenever possible, students should provide duplicate copies of supporting documentation in their portfolio and keep the originals archived (this may not be possible with works of art). The supporting documentation collected by the student can include both direct and indirect sources:

Direct sources—original work created, produced, written, designed, or composed by a student. Examples include reports, Web sites, computer designs, art objects, or videos of performances.

Indirect sources—documents produced by others that support or attest to a student's learning. Indirect sources might include certificates, meeting minutes, testimonies, performance evaluations, articles, contracts, or letters of verification.

Depending on the subject matter of the petition, students should use a combination of direct and indirect sources for supporting documentation.

What Is the Purpose of Using Supporting Documentation?

1. Supporting documentation provides evidence of learning, level of learning, and whether the learning is current. The supporting documentation should help evaluators make credit decisions. Therefore, supporting documentation provides evidence to back up the student's claims.

2. Supporting documentation helps colleges meet accreditation standards for assessment by showing that the evidence of the learning is accurate and that the student is responsible for the work claimed. Verification letters should be from credible sources who have firsthand knowledge of the experiential learning a student claims and should be written on letterhead.

3. Supporting documentation demonstrates a student's critical-thinking ability. Since compiling supporting documentation and obtaining letters of verification takes time and thought, it provides further evidence of a student's ability to think critically about his or her learning.

How Do I Begin the Process of Gathering Supporting Documentation?

A good starting point is to consider what to gather and who could assist you. Often, finding one document leads to finding another.

As you begin to gather materials, consider the following questions:

- Do you have business cards, job descriptions, work products, or performance reviews from your job positions?
- What work-related training or development have you had? Do you have records or certificates? Can you obtain records from a human resource department? Do you have outlines, programs, or certificates of completion from a course, workshop, seminar, conference, or training

BOX 11.1 Critical Thinking about Supporting Documentation

Describe the supporting documentation you've gathered. Why did you save this document or artifact? What are the best samples you could use to demonstrate your learning? Why are they the best?

program? Did you obtain a government clearance or clear a criminal background check?

- Have you completed non-credit courses or independent studies? Have you completed courses that were not accepted for transfer credit (possibly due to accreditation standards)? Can you obtain transcripts or course descriptions?
- Have you participated in workshops, seminars, or conferences?
- Have you received awards, trophies, certificates, commendations, or letters of appreciation?
- Have you been licensed—for example, received a broker's, appraiser's, financial, contractor's, or real estate license?
- Do you have artistic or musical ability that can be supported with documentation or exhibits of paintings, jewelry, pottery, musical scores, programs, or photos?
- Do you have videos or CDs of performances such as dance, sign language interpretation, or speeches?
- Do you have photos of finished work, travel to other countries, missions, or volunteer trips?
- Have you volunteered extensively or developed hobbies that can be verified?
- Do you have documentation of your spiritual journey, such as notes from Bible studies, training, or documents that verify your experience?
- From whom or where could you find copies of records?
- Who observed your work?
- Do you have a family member, friend, or co-worker who could help you locate supporting documentation?
- Do you have the names of supervisors who can write letters of verification to include in your documentation?

BOX 11.2 Types of Supporting Documentation

Artwork	Licenses
Articles	Manuals
Awards	Meeting minutes
Bibliographies (annotated) of reading	Musical scores
	Patents
Brochures	Performance appraisals or reviews
Budgets	Photos
Bulletin boards (photos)	PowerPoint® slides
Business cards	Presentation or meeting feedback forms
Business correspondence	
Certificates of training	Professional letters
Computer coding	Programs
Conference descriptions	Proposals
Contracts	Real estate records
Corporate announcements	Reports
Creative writing (such as plays, poems, and stories)	Software programs
	Spreadsheets
Curriculum and lesson plans	Surveys
Graphics	Video or audio tape
Job descriptions	Web sites
Letters from satisfied customers	Workshop descriptions
Letters of verification of the learning	Writing

How Should I Select Supporting Documentation?

Supporting documentation should be relevant to the subject matter.

The document should relate to the learning outcomes described in the course or competency. The evaluator should be able to recognize the connection between the learning and the supporting documentation. When in doubt, a student should ask whether a document verifies the claims to the learning. Weak examples of documentation include general articles or announcements without a student's name or connection to the student's learning.

Supporting documentation should be authentic.

The evidence used must be truthful representations of a student's learning. Letters of verification can testify that a student produced the work alone or with a team as well as the level of knowledge, skills, and abilities involved. Students should always be open and honest about their contributions to projects.

Supporting documentation should represent the best samples.

When selecting supporting documentation, quality is more important than quantity. For instance, one or two of the best samples of written work such as lesson plans, newsletters, or computer codes are better than multiple samples. If a student wrote a manual, several sample pages and a letter of verification attesting to his or her authorship would be sufficient.

When choosing samples, students should always keep the audience in mind. Evaluators are busy and not impressed when students pad the portfolio with irrelevant or redundant samples. When selecting items, remember that one document may demonstrate learning in a number of areas and can be cross-referenced in the narrative or competency statements. "Don't overwhelm me by padding the portfolio with extraneous documents," said one evaluator (Zizzi, M., personal communication, April 5, 2005).

What Are Letters of Verification?

A letter of verification provides validation of a student's knowledge, skills, and abilities related to the areas being petitioned in the portfolio. The letter-writer must have firsthand knowledge of a student's work and level of expertise. The letter verifies the learning, so it differs from a letter of appreciation or commendation. In addition, the letter should be written by a reliable and credible source such as an employer or expert. The letter should not be written by a friend or family member. The letter of verification is typically written on letterhead and signed by the author.

What Are Some Tips for Requesting Letters of Verification?

Students should start the process of soliciting letters early and monitor their requests by using a calendar or checklist with the date of the request and date received. One effective way to request letters is to call the writer first, and follow the conversation with specifics on the purpose and contents in an e-mail.

BOX 11.3   Letters of Verification

A high-quality letter of verification includes:

1. Author's credentials, relationship to the student, and dates observed.
2. Description of the "duties, responsibilities, and tasks involved in the experiential learning under consideration" (Whitaker, 1989, p. 58).
3. Summary or list of the learning (knowledge, skills, and abilities) achieved as a result of performing these duties.
4. Statement that attests to the performance level based on one or more of the following factors:
   - level of learning demonstrated compared to others in a known reference group (e.g., average, above average, superior)
   - level of development observed (e.g., progress from novice to expert)
   - level of performance comparable to a college-level course (if needed, students can provide information for the writer on the course or competencies under consideration)
   - level of transferability of the skills (i.e., highly transferable skills would mean the skill sets acquired would easily transfer to other jobs or projects)
5. The letter should be signed, dated, and printed on letterhead.

The following sample shows a letter of verification request by e-mail.

BOX 11.4   Sample Letter of Verification Request by E-mail

Subject line: Letter needed by 11/22

Dear _____

As a follow-up to our conversation, I am requesting a verification letter to include in my prior learning portfolio. The purpose of the letter is to verify my experiential learning and the level of learning I achieved in the areas described below.

(continued)

Please include the following elements in the letter:

1. State your title, relationship to me, and dates observed. For reference, you supervised my work at the company from 7/2000–9/2004.

2. Provide a short description of the duties I performed alone or as a team. Attest that I worked as a customer service assistant and then a customer services team leader.

3. Provide a brief summary of the knowledge, skills, and abilities I demonstrated in the following areas: (name competencies associated with the coursework being petitioned)

4. Attest to the level at which I performed these competencies (average, above average, superior). Attest to the level of my competency compared to a lower-division course. I am petitioning for credits toward my elective category for the degree.

5. Include any other statements that would help an evaluator determine what skills I demonstrated when I performed as a team leader.

6. The letter should be signed, dated, and printed on letterhead.

Please mail the letter to me at (provide address) or I will pick up the letter on (date).

Thank you in advance for your help as I pursue my educational goals of achieving my bachelor's degree in business administration. Please e-mail or phone me with any questions.

Sincerely,

(Name, title, address, e-mail address, phone number)

What is a Statement of Authenticity?

A statement of authenticity attests to the authenticity of the claim. There are two types of statements of authenticity:

1. Student signature that indicates that the student is responsible for the work presented and that all supporting documentation is an accurate and true representation.

2. Statements on letterhead by another person who testifies that the work presented is an accurate and true representation of a student's work. In cases where a student has worked on a project as a team, the statement indicates the level of contribution from the student.

What Materials Are Useful for Compiling Supporting Documentation?

Students should follow their college's guidelines. The following are some materials typically used by portfolio students:

1. Archival storage for originals: Store all original supporting documentation in a storage folder or box that can be divided into categories. Electronic documents can be backed up on a disc or CD-ROM or memory stick. Do not laminate documents.
2. Binder: Use a three-ring binder or small three-ring binders (if the portfolio is divided by subject matter). D-ring binders help supporting documentation lay flat. Zippered binders are best if including supporting documentation such as a CD-ROM.
3. Clear sheet protectors (if required by the college).
4. Section dividers or tabs.
5. Two-sided tape.
6. Labels.
7. Yellow highlighter: If needed, students should use a yellow highlighter or other method to draw the attention to the sentences or sections of a document that are relevant to the learning outcomes. For example, a sentence in a performance review can be highlighted to draw attention to the section that verifies the student's skills and abilities.

Avoid: Sticky notes, paper clips, or anything that could fall off the pages of the portfolio.

What Are Some Tips for Compiling Supporting Documentation?

Advice from Amy Dressel-Martin of Dressel-Martin MediaWorks Inc. on preparing professional-looking supporting documentation (personal communication, February 9, 2005).

- Use either bold or underlining for captions (don't mix the two).
- Use easy-to-read fonts such as Times or Times New Roman.
- Use a consistent format (paper, type, style, and headings).
- Use a high-quality printer or copier to print out or make copies of documents. If needed, trim and use correction fluid to clean up documents before copying.
- Use black ink.
- Check for spelling and grammatical errors.
- Use plastic sleeves, if allowed (use non-glare sleeves, if available).
- Keep the pages clean and uncluttered. Place one or two items on a page.
- Use one-inch margins on pages.
- Use high-quality white paper for documents such as resumés.
- Place photos on the left side of the page and put captions on the right, or center the caption and photo on the page.
- Clip and photocopy articles with the dateline and publication intact on the first page of the article, or cut the dateline and publication and tape the information on top of the page with the article below before copying.
- Avoid using clip art or stickers (exception: graphic artist or teacher education portfolio).

How Do I Organize and Reference My Supporting Documentation?

Prepare an index to documents on a separate page that lists all sources of documentations. If needed, provide an explanation if a caption does not describe the document. Normally, supporting documentation is numbered in the order discussed in the narrative or competency statement. Or the supporting documentation can be listed thematically or chronologically. Commonly, students use tabs or section dividers so evaluators can easily turn to the correct supporting documentation. When referencing supporting documentation in a narrative or competency statement, put the parenthesis before the final punctuation in a sentence, as follows:

I created a bulletin board for social studies students to provide a visual representation of the timeline of events (see photo in Document 3).

In the next two positions, I wrote performance evaluations for my employ-ees (refer to sample 4.1 and 4.2 and verification letter in Document 5).

I revised the human resource benefits publication several times and re-ceived an accommodation from my employer for my efforts (refer to Document 5).

What Are Captions, and How Do I Write Effective Captions?

Captions provide a brief explanation of the document. A good caption in-corporates the "five Ws": who, what, why, where, and when. If the process of creating the supporting documentation is particularly relevant, a student could add an explanation of "how." Effective captions are accurate and spelled correctly. If there are several items on a page or people in a photo, the caption should identify the items from left to right.

Depending on the college's requirements, captions can be included on an index page or typed and printed on a label and adhered to the copy of the document or the plastic sheet protector. If needed, the caption can pro-vide an explanation of the relevance of the document to a specific learn-ing outcome. In addition, captions can be used to show evidence of im-provement, or steps taken to gain competency. The following sample captions show how adding specifics can make the caption more useful for the evaluators.

BOX 11.5   Writing Captions

Before: The photo above shows me accepting an award.

Better: Document 3. The photo (above) was taken in September of 2004 when I received an award from the Nonprofit Center of Colorado for my work in planning, writing, and producing a resource directory.

Before: Certificate in JAVA script.

Better: Supporting documentation 8 and 9. In November of 2004, I attended a two-week intensive course on JAVA programming, which was sponsored by the Computer Training Institute and attended by myself and employees of Systems, Inc. The course description and course topics, shown to the right, were retrieved and printed from the Computer Training Institute's Web site.

(continued)

Before: Before and after samples.

Better: Supporting documentation 6 and 7—before and after samples of business writing.

Before: The document on the left side of the page is an excerpt from the company request document I wrote in September of 2003 (names blacked out to protect privacy). This written request was too lengthy and disorganized.

Better: The document on the right, which I wrote in November of 2004, demonstrates the competencies I gained in business writing, including attention to the audience, clear organization, and proper editing.

How Many Pieces of Supporting Documentation Do I Need?

The number depends on the college's requirements and the subject matter. For example, teacher education portfolios may require a variety of supporting documentation such as letters, lesson plans, student papers, and training records. Many schools recommend approximately five pieces of supporting documentation for each three-credit course being petitioned. In all cases, "excessive documentation, attractively presented, should not compensate for poor performance in assessment . . ." (Whitaker, 1989, p. 58).

What If I Am Having Trouble Locating Supporting Documentation?

First, students who have the learning should write a thorough narrative or competency statement that attest with enough detail to their knowledge, skills, and abilities. In addition, while writing the narrative or competency statements, students often uncover potential supporting documentation and sources that will verify their learning. Often writing the narrative triggers ideas for supporting documentation that verifies the learning such as business cards, brochures, job descriptions, or certificates.

Second, students may be able to find a current e-mail address or contact information from former employers by using Internet search engines (such as www.switchboard.com) and request letters of verification.

Third, in some instances, students can reproduce their original work. For instance, if a student could not locate the outline for a speech given several years earlier, he or she could create the outline. Indirect documentation such as job descriptions, flyers, or letter of validation could verify that the student presented the speech.

Fourth, in cases where information is proprietary, students should include an explanation about why the document is not included or information is blacked out (see the following questions on proprietary information).

Fifth, if the learning is not verifiable with supporting documentation, students might consider other assessment methods. It is always advisable to discuss these challenges with a portfolio specialist.

Are the Contents of My Portfolio and the Documents Kept Confidential?

The portfolio contents will only be reviewed by a faculty member and the evaluator(s). Portfolio contents are not shared with the general public. If concerned, students can ask the college for their confidentiality statement or policy on confidentiality. Portfolios are not shared with other students unless the author provides a written release (personal information and company names are generally blacked out before the contents are shown to other students). Students should take precautions when using proprietary information (see next question).

What Is Proprietary Information, and How Do I Protect Proprietary Information in My Supporting Documentation?

Propriety information is "material and information relating to or associated with a company's products, business, or activities, including, but not limited to, financial information; data or statements; trade secrets; product research and development; existing and future product designs and performance specifications; marketing plans or techniques; schematics; client lists; computer programs; processes; and know-how that has been clearly identified and properly marked by the company as proprietary information, trade secrets, or company confidential information" (ATIS, 2000, para. 1).

Protecting Proprietary Information

- Obtain permission to use any documents that have been identified as proprietary information, trade secrets, or company confidential information.

- Black out proprietary information such as names, dates, e-mails, and project findings on documents by using a black marker or white-out tape, and then photocopying the document.
- Black out faces of children in classroom settings, if advised, to protect privacy.
- Find indirect sources that do not reveal proprietary information.
- Write captions to explain the circumstances.
- Obtain a letter, if needed, to verify the authenticity of the work.

What Are Some Tips for Using an Electronic Portfolio?

Some colleges provide password-protected electronic portfolios (also known as e-portfolios, Webfolios, and digital portfolios), which are commonly used to build career portfolios, demonstrate writing, or show competencies in teacher education programs. Batson (2002) defines an electronic portfolio as a "dynamic Web site that interfaces with a database of student work artifacts" (para. 8).

Depending on the storage space, students can add scanned documents, audio, video clips, slide presentations, and graphics. Digital cameras allow students to capture photographic images of evidence such as art pieces or bulletin boards on disc, and then upload photos to a server. The advantages of using an e-portfolio include easy storage and portability. Even though the sites are password protected, students are never guaranteed absolute privacy on the Internet. Loading word-processing documents on an e-portfolio site is not difficult, but scanning and loading supporting documentation can present some challenges. Documents that are difficult to decipher, when scanned, may require a caption to explain the contents.

The following are e-portfolio guidelines from Elise Sweet, a portfolio specialist at Regis University (personal communication, February 19, 2005):

- Download and print the portfolio guides. Learn the software requirements and storage capacity. The space requirements may limit the amount of supporting documentation or supporting documentation.
- Create and archive supporting documentation in electronic form. Use a zip disk or CD-RW disk or organize supporting documentation in folders and subfolders on a hard drive.
- Review requirements for scanned documents. Be sure the scanned document is readable when uploaded.

Students should always consider the needs and software capabilities of the evaluators when building an electronic portfolio. In addition, students should always re-check their e-portfolio to make sure that items are organized logically and loaded properly.

What Are Some Tips for Submitting My Portfolio?

1. Create a submission checklist of items that you will include in your portfolio (or one that the college has provided). Re-check that all the contents are included. It is easy to leave out an item such as a letter of validation that hasn't arrived.
2. Always keep back-up copies of every item in the portfolio in an archive.
3. Submit the portfolio by the deadline.
4. Check that contents are edited, organized, and professional looking, but don't overdo the formatting. Remember that the purpose of your portfolio is to demonstrate learning. It can be tempting to spend too much time arranging supporting documentation while neglecting to prepare high-quality narratives or competency statements.
5. Arrange for pick-up or delivery of the portfolio. Since proper assessment takes time, it is advisable for students to check in advance how long the assessment process normally takes before calling for the results.

Adult Learner Profiles

See Appendices 6–8 for samples and excerpts from Maria's narrative and documentation. See Appendix 8 for a sample of a letter of verification from Maria's supervisor.

See Appendix 5 for a sample of Tim's table of contents and supporting documentation index. Tim carefully blacked out proprietary information and received permission from his boss to use the material.

REVIEW

- Finding the best supporting documentation to demonstrate your learning requires critical thinking.
- Letters are a form of documentation used to verify that the learning has taken place.

- Captions help explain the nature of the document and the reason for its inclusion.
- Take appropriate measures to protect proprietary information.
- When using an electronic portfolio, supporting documentation can be scanned and uploaded.

NEXT STEPS

1. Locate, arrange, and provide captions for supporting documentation.
2. Follow the requirements for submitting the portfolio to the appropriate office for assessment.

REFERENCES

ATIS Telecom. American National Standard Glossary. (2000). Retrieved October 20, 2004, from http://www.atis.org/tg2k/.

Batson, T. (2002, December 1). The Electronic Portfolio Boom: What's It All About? *Syllabus.* Retrieved October 7, 2004, from http://www.campus-technology.com/article.asp?id=6984.

Rodrigues, E. (July 24, 2005). It's never too late, older students say. *Miami Herald.* Retrieved September 3, 2005: www.miami.com/mld/miamiherald/living/special_packages/backtoschool/12198485.htm.

Whitaker, U. (1989). *Assessing Learning: Standards, Principles, and Procedures.* Chicago: CAEL.

FINAL REMARKS

Many adult students who return to school have survived the threats of downsizing and restructuring. They've recognized the need for retraining or a degree but are fearful about returning to school. Through prior learning assessment, students gain confidence in their ability to perform at the college level. In addition, they are able to earn credit for their skills, knowledge, and abilities.

Keep in mind these important points when undertaking the PLA process:

- Determine a goal and make an academic plan
- Receive information and guidance on the college's methods and policies for the assessment of prior learning
- Reflect during and after experiences to maximize learning opportunities

- Appreciate how writing about learning leads to new learning
- Budget time to fully benefit from assessment methods such as portfolio development

An article in the June 24, 2005, *Miami Herald* is titled "It's never too late, older students say. College students in their 70s, 80s, even 90s are finding pleasure in a return to school." Learning does not stop in high school, or even at midlife. Learning is a lifelong activity.

Note from the Author

Receiving credit through prior learning assessment is an effective catalyst for students who are determined to complete a college degree. As of this date, "Andrew" completed his doctorate and is teaching at a university. "Tim" received the raise he desired; and "Maria" is now close to completing her bachelor's degree and teacher licensure. I hope that this book will inspire other students to earn college credit for what they know.

Janet Colvin

Appendices

APPENDIX 1

Finding Institutions That Offer Prior Learning Assessment

Students can use several methods for locating institutions that offer prior learning assessment.

Find a college or university that offers the program or major you are seeking (e.g., www.petersons.com has a searchable database).

1. Locate a college's Web site. Use the search function to locate prior learning assessment. Often prior learning assessment is mentioned in the instructions for the admissions process.

2. Call a college or university to find out if it offers prior learning assessment. For instance:
   - Andrew enrolled in the adult learning program at his local college and found out about prior learning assessment during the admissions process.
   - Tim was directed to the testing office and then to the department for adult learner services.
   - Maria initially inquired at a four-year institution and was referred to the local community college.

3. If available, use e-mail to reply to the "Contact Us" feature on a school's (or adult learning program's) Web site to inquire about prior learning assessment options.

4. Ask an admissions or marketing representative or advisor at the college if prior learning assessment services are available.

5. If a college does not offer a portfolio assessment program, find out if the college you attend will accept transfer credits earned through prior learning assessment from another institution. Often colleges have agreements with local colleges that provide portfolio assessment programs. Students may have to register for a portfolio or prior learning assessment course through the partnering institution and then transfer the credit.

6. Search for adult learning programs on the Internet or use one of the key words or phrases listed below:
    - Prior learning assessment
    - Credit options
    - Assessment of prior learning
    - Learning from experience
    - Challenge exams
    - Credit by examination
    - Testing
    - Admissions
    - Experiential learning
    - Adult learning or professional studies

    Departments that may house prior learning assessment services:
    - Advising
    - Admissions
    - Student services
    - Registrar
    - Testing
    - Prior learning assessment services
    - Career counseling

The assessment of prior learning may be listed under a number of names:

Prior Learning Assessment (PLA)

Prior Learning Assessment and Recognition (PLAR—Canadian)

Assessment of Prior Learning or Flexible Assessment (APL—UK)

Recognition of Prior Learning (RPL—Australian and South African)

Assessment and Recognition of Prior Learning and Experience (ARPLE)

Assessment of Prior Certified Learning (APCL)

Accreditation of Prior Experiential Learning (APEL)

To locate colleges that offer CLEP and DSST testing sites, visit:

CLEP Web site: http://www.collegeboard.com
DSST Web site: http://www.getcollegecredit.com

To locate colleges that recognize ACE credit recommendations, visit:

http://www.acenet.edu

APPENDIX 2

Prior Learning Inventory

Adult learners often have a variety of learning experiences, including college credit courses, workshops and seminars, certifications, and workplace learning. The purpose of the prior learning inventory is to list your experiences, training, and learning competencies that may be useful for assessment planning. This information will be helpful for planning your education as well as beginning to determine the college-level learning and what methods of prior learning assessment to explore. The information gathered for this process will help you organize your experiences and learning. This information will also help an academic advisor or prior learning specialist assist you in developing an effective educational plan. If you decide to write a portfolio, the information will be essential for developing the document.

Create a Folder

Start by creating a folder in a location on your computer that is easy to access, or use a paper filing system. As you complete the prior learning inventory and, subsequently, the exercises in this book, save each document to this folder. Label your folder "Prior Learning Inventory" or a similar name that is easy to identify.

The documents you save in your folder include:

Part 1—Prior Learning Inventory—An inventory of your experiences.
Part 2—List of Skills—A list of the general skills and categories that match your learning.
Part 3—Competencies—A list of the competencies you have obtained from your experience.

PART 1 Prior Learning Inventory

Instructions:

1. State your experiences in each category.
2. Follow each category with details, including dates (can be approximate), type of experience, and a brief description.
3. Skip sections that do not apply.
4. Update your inventory as needed.

Categories:

1. Name and identification information
   Include: name, address, work and home phone numbers, e-mail address(es), fax number, student i.d. or social security number
2. High school
   State your high school information.
   Include: name of school, dates of attendance, type (diploma or GED)
2. Education after high school
   Include: dates, school, Web site, concentration or types of courses completed
3. Military service
   Include: branch, date entered, date discharged, rank
   Optional: military training, schools, type/length of training, occupational specialty, brief description of types of military assignments
4. Languages
   Include: language, fluency level (beginning, advanced), spoken or written (or both)
5. Professional training
   (non-credit courses and independent studies, distance courses workshops, seminars and conferences, training programs, certifications or examinations passed)
   Include: dates, title, school or sponsor, type of training
6. Employment history
   Include: dates, company name, type of business, job titles, job duties, location
   Optional: insert the section of your resume that lists employment history (include supervisors' names, addresses, e-mail addresses)
7. Professional societies or organizations
   Include: dates, names, membership held, offices held, committees, service

(continued)

8. Original work
   (written documents such as original reports, articles, grants, technical manuals, marketing materials, copyrights, Web sites, and intranets prepared either by you or a team)
   Include: dates, companies, and brief description
9. Computer or technical expertise
   Include: dates, type of training, software skills, and computer languages, level of mastery (beginning, intermediate, advanced)
10. Civic or political organizations or activities
    Include: dates, organizations, brief descriptions of duties
11. Volunteer activities
    Include: dates, organizations, brief descriptions of duties
12. Sports and recreational pursuits
    Include: dates, type, level of expertise, training received
13. Artistic pursuits
    (artistic ability and knowledge, skills, appreciation of the arts)
    Include: dates, type, brief description of artistic works or artist's portfolio
14. History, cultural, or regional studies
    (knowledge of history, travel, cultures, region, anthropology, or geography)
    Include: dates, type, brief descriptions
15. Religious and spiritual activities
    (training, memberships, reading, courses, small groups, retreats, committees served, missions, self-help programs, or recovery programs)
    Include: dates, sponsor, and brief descriptions
16. Accomplishments
    (inventions or patents, commendations, honors or promotions, trophies, letters of appreciation, or recognitions)
    Include: dates, organization, brief descriptions

Transcript checklist:
List transcripts and records requested. Include college transcripts, ACE, and military records (see Chapter 5 for more details).
Include: type of transcript, date requested

PART 2   Categories of Skills

From the list below, what general skills and categories best match your areas of learning?

LIST OF GENERAL SKILLS AND CATEGORIES:

Accounting	Graphics	Project management
Advertising	History	Public relations
Art	Hotel	Public speaking
Broadcasting	Hospitality	Purchasing
Business	Horticultural	Quality control
Business software	Human resources	Real estate
Buyer	Human services	Retail
Communication	Insurance	Research
Computer	Intercultural	Safety
programming	Interpersonal	Sales
Conflict resolution	Interviewing	Science
Construction	Investigation	Social work
Counseling	Journalism	Small business
Customer service	Labor relations	Spiritual
Database	Language	Sports
management	Leadership	Supervision
Design	Legal	Teambuilding
Drafting	Literacy	Technical support
Education	Managing	Telecommunication
Economics	Marketing	Trade
Engineering	Medical	Training
Environmental	Music	Volunteer work
science	Nutrition	Web design
Financial	Nonprofit	Writing
Fire science	Office administration	Other _____
Fundraising	Police training	

PART 3   List of Competencies

For each category described in Part 2, specify the skills and competencies you obtained. Many skills, such as managing projects, involve both people and data.

PEOPLE SKILLS	INFORMATION/ DATA SKILLS	DOING SKILLS
Appreciating (diversity, styles, differences)	Analyzing	Adjusting
	Applying	Assembling
	Budgeting	Building
Coaching	Clarifying	Calculating
Communicating	Composing	Coding
Consulting	Computing	Completing tasks
Coordinating	Conceptualizing	Constructing
Creating	Data collecting	Creating (visual arts)
Delegating	Decision-making	Delivering
Evaluating	Developing ideas	Demonstrating
Facilitating	Editing	Designing
Handling conflict	Estimating	Driving/operating
Helping	Evaluating	Engineering
Relaying information	Examining	Growing
	Formulating	Handling
Leading	Gathering	Inventing
Listening	Handling logistics	Making things
Managing conflict	Investigating	Manipulating
Mediating	Learning	Manufacturing
Mentoring	Managing projects	Operating equipment
Mobilizing	Observing	Producing
Motivating	Organizing	Repairing
Negotiating	Problem-solving	Tuning
Performing	Reading for information	Using numbers, software programs, tools, materials
Presenting	Reporting	
Recruiting	Researching	Working with
Satisfying customers	Scheduling tasks	_____
Selling	Setting procedures	
Supervising	Sorting	
Teaching	Strategizing	
Team-building	Streamlining	
Training	Structuring	
Understanding	Studying	
	Supplying	
	Synthesizing	
	Testing quality	
	Visualizing	
	Writing	

APPENDIX 3

U.S. and International Accreditation

For U.S. schools, accreditation is recognized by the Council on Higher Education Accreditation (CHEA), which is online at www.chea.org.

The six regional accrediting institutions include:

Middle State Association of Colleges and Schools
www.msache.org

New England Association of Schools and Colleges
www.neasc.org

North Central Association of Colleges and Schools
www.ncacihe.org

Northwest Association of Schools and Colleges
www.cocnasc.org

Southern Association of Colleges and Schools
www.sacs.org

Western Association of Schools and Colleges
www.wascweb.org

Schools in Great Britain and the British Commonwealth must be members of the Association of Commonwealth Universities and must have a listing in the Commonwealth Universities Yearbook.

Schools in Australia must be recognized by the Australian Qualifications Framework.

Schools not covered by the aforementioned accrediting bodies must be in either the World Education Series (published by Projects for International Education Research (PIER)) or in the Country Series (published by Australia's National Office for Overseas Skills Recognition).

John Bear, author of *Bears' Guide to Earning Degrees by Distance Learning* (15th ed., Ten Speed Press, 2003), utilizes the generally accepted accrediting principles (GAAP) to determine which schools are accredited.

APPENDIX 4

Military Transcripts and Resources

Requesting military transcripts:

http://aarts.army.mil/
Army and National Guard reservists and veterans
AARTS transcripts

https://smart.cnet.navy.mil/
Navy and Marine Corps
SMART transcript

http://www.au.af.mil/au/ccaf/
Community College of the Air Force
(See "Transcript" on the Navigational Tool Bar)

http://www.uscg.mil/hq/cgi/
U.S. Coast Guard Institute

Additional military resources:

http://militaryguides.acenet.edu/
ACE military recommendation service

www.military.com
Information on obtaining transcripts from each branch of the military
(Click on the "Education" link on the navigational bar)

www.gibill.va.gov
Information on the G.I. Bill and Veterans Administration benefits from the
U.S. Government

www.soc.aascu.org/
Information on Service Members Opportunity Colleges, a consortium of
colleges and universities dedicated to helping service members and their
families obtain college degrees

APPENDIX 5

Sample Table of Contents for a Portfolio of Prior Learning Assessment

Adult learner profile: Tim
Prior learning assessment portfolio

Table of Contents

APPENDIX 6

Sample Cover Sheet and Narrative Excerpt

Course Description Research and Prewriting Strategies

Communication Narrative and Competency Statements

Introduction to Communication (3) COM 101 Lower Division
Provides an overview of communication and the competencies necessary to communicate effectively in today's society. Students will enhance their communication skills in interpersonal, small group, and public speaking settings.

Key Terms and Concepts

To assist Maria in the identification of the key concepts, Maria found an "Introduction to Communication" textbook at her college library.

Here is her preliminary list of topics to study based on her reading and analysis of the textbook:

Public speaking:

- Nonverbal and verbal elements
- Organization
- Visual aids
- Adapting to the audience

Interpersonal communication:

- Listening
- Perception
- Empathy
- Identity and culture
- Conflict resolution

Small groups:

- Roles and responsibilities
- Ground rules
- Facilitation
- Leadership styles

The sample below is excerpted from a section of Maria's portfolio.

- This excerpt shows her demonstration of learning in communication in narrative format (Appendix 6).
- A second sample shows her demonstration of learning in communication in a three-column format (Appendix 7).
- Students should select the format recommended by the college.

SAMPLE   Portfolio Cover Sheet and Statement of Authenticity

Portfolio for Prior Learning Assessment
[*Fill in name of college and office*]
Submitted to Community College
Adult Learning Assessment Office

Petition for requirements for the degree:
[*Degree or goal*]
[*Current Month, Day, Year*]

[Name]
[Student ID number]
[Address]
[Day and Evening Phone Numbers]
[Fax Number]
[E-mail Address]

Signature and Statement of Authenticity
I, *[full name]*, certify that the information in this portfolio and the supporting documentation submitted is true, accurate, and represents my original work.

_____ (signature)   _____ (date)

Sample: Narrative Format

Introduction

Note: Maria's supporting documentation is not included in this book. The narrative is fictional but is based on several students' experiences.

In this prior learning portfolio, I will discuss my learning from being a wife and mother, in-home day care provider, employee at a domestic violence shelter, and assistant teacher at Head Start. I will also discuss how my experience as a Latina woman and educator has shaped my life. After writing my learning autobiography, I realized that I have learned more than my credentials will show. I have attended First Aid and CPR courses from the American Red Cross. I have attended training and a literacy conference through my Head Start program. However, what my credentials don't show is the lessons I've learned from many other life and work experiences. This narrative will demonstrate my learning.

In Spanish we have a saying that describes how I got along with my mother in my early adult years, it was "like water and oil" (which don't mix). Since maturing, I've appreciated how my Mom pushed me and her other seven children to get an education. My goal is to obtain my associate's degree in Early Childhood education. And, that is just the beginning. When I graduate, I want to enter the combined bachelor's and master's degree program.

I will discuss in this narrative my learning related to the following subject areas: communication, cultural studies, early childhood teaching methods, first aid, and piano. The discussion that follows will be primarily about my learning in the first three subjects. The First Aid will be documented with certificates and a brief explanation. The piano experience is documented with a video tape with me teaching children piano. In Section 3, I've included an index to my documents followed by the documents I'm using to support my petition for credit.

Topic 1: Introduction to Communication

Introduction to Communication (3) COM 101 Lower Division
Provides an overview of communication and the competencies necessary to communicate effectively in today's society. Students will enhance their communication skills in public speaking, interpersonal, and small group settings.

Introduction

My mother insisted we speak and write English at home, so I grew up hearing Spanish and would defiantly respond to my mother and father's scolding in Spanish. Today, as a bilingual educator, communication is an essential part of my work. I have used communication skills in many settings, both at home and at work. When I was a day care provider, I had to communicate with my parents on the needs of the children and the schedule. I used nonverbal communication with the babies and children to communicate a nurturing environment. When I worked in a domestic violence shelter, I had training on handling crisis calls and listening to clients during intakes. And, I even spoke in public with my knees knocking and my palms sweating. Now, I work in groups with 3-, 4-, and 5-year-old Latino children teaching literacy and other skills. I continually learn at work and at home how to improve my skills. Communication is very important in building marriages and working on teams. Without my experience and mentors who helped me to improve my communication skills, I would have not pursued my dream to be an early childhood teacher. In this narrative, I will describe my experiential learning related to the following communication settings: public speaking, interpersonal communication, and small group communication.

Public Speaking

Public speaking is hard, but once I did more and more, I got more confident. I could speak to a group of parents or a group of children, but speaking in front of a public audience was scary. I saw the PowerPoint presentations people made and they looked so professional. My supervisor at the shelter informed me that we received a grant that included education in the schools with teens, children, and parents. I had to pick up my nerve and do it. I was nervous about setting up audio visual equipment, so I just started with simple visual aids and handouts. I know that I talked too fast. So, when I was in a classroom I tried to remember to breathe and slow down to the pace of a creek, not a river. One time, I talked to second graders about friendship and using words to handle disagreements. They looked at me so sweetly, that I smiled and relaxed. From then on, I started to like to speak with more confidence.

When I got better at organizing my ideas, I started with a fresh introduction, a body, and a conclusion that was geared to that audience's age. For young children, I discussed friendship, conflict resolution, and using words to talk about problems. We even did role plays so the kids were involved. I talked about domestic violence myths to teens. I separated the girls because I noticed the boys would snicker and make rude remarks. I tried to be sensitive to the teacher's needs and preferences because I was presenting to a high school psychology class. The teacher told me that the teens liked the presentation I did, and there was good discussion. With adults, I allowed questions. Some of the questions surprised me because I didn't think the audience was always paying attention. I got better and better at involving audience participation and created a game, a poster, and scenarios. That way, I wasn't just doing all the talking. One time I prepared a hand-out with two spelling errors. After a teacher pointed it out, I was careful to review my materials. I gave at least 20 speeches one year and adapted it to all different ages and types of audiences.

Then, finally, it was time to try PowerPoint. It was easier to use than I thought. We had to meet with the grant committee and I wanted to be professional. I kept in mind the purpose: to inform the committee about how we used the funding we received and to persuade them about the need for future spending. I put the facts on slides and used graphics with two charts to show our numbers. I practiced so much and I was thinking about my speech all the time as if I was a president giving an address. I tried to consciously eliminate "um"s because I used them when I was nervous. I prepared an introduction with a statistic on the prevalence of domestic violence, so they would know why our program was important. I used seven slides, which was about right for the 10 minutes (see outline and slides in Document 3). I wanted to present the facts since they were looking for the numbers. I dressed professionally. I was glad that I learned to be calm. I talked to the panel and I looked at them respectfully. I received applause and questions. When I didn't know an answer to a question on statistics on the diversity of the populations we served, I said I'd get back to them because I knew it was in the report but I didn't want to waste the panel's time thumbing through pages. I always told the truth. Later, I was told that we received re-funding and I'm proud of that.

My experience in the Head Start classroom has helped me to project my voice without yelling. We use several classroom management techniques to get the children to look and listen. I also have to show assertiveness because especially when we are out on field trips or buses, I must have control of the children. When I lead music with the children, I always wait to get their attention first. I use my eyes when I'm playing the piano to look at the children who are off task. We use our bodies to communicate time and rhythm through clapping, stomping, and dance. I also have learned that transitions between activities have to be managed with music or a simple movement. I couldn't allow dead space. Nonverbal messages are very powerful.

Once I learned to manage my nervousness, I enjoyed giving speeches. It is hard to believe that this shy girl could speak in public. Over this year in my college classes, I had to give speeches as well. I noticed that some of the students just read their notes. At one time, I read my speeches. Now,

I use note cards with key words on the organization of my speeches. I convinced my group on a group project in class to use PowerPoint with just the main ideas and some simple graphics. Our presentation was well received. Speaking is now one of my strengths. I am still getting better at using transitions from one of my points to another because I like to tell stories and can get off track. I remind myself to stay on the topic or I will confuse my audience. It also has helped to watch my teachers who are prepared and knowledgeable. I look forward to more public speaking experiences as a teacher.

Supporting Documentation

Document 1—Letter from supervisor
Document 3—Statistics on the number of presentations
Document 4—Text of speech and PowerPoint miniatures
Document 8—Performance evaluation

Interpersonal Communication

Interpersonal communication is a "dynamic process between or among people that touches people emotionally and psychologically" (Miller & Steinberg, 1975, p. 6). It is most associated with one-on-one communication. Interpersonal communication builds relationships or can tear them down. Interpersonal communication is different and more complex than "impersonal" communication. I use e-mail to get my work schedule and respond to simple messages which are primarily simple "impersonal" messages. I use face-to-face interpersonal communication in my work with students, parents, and family members to build more meaningful relationships.

I learned about escalation and de-escalation of conflict during a difficult situation when a perpetrator found our shelter and stopped me when I was getting out of my car to start my shift. The man threatened to burn down the shelter unless I got his wife. I sat the man down first and I told him that I understood that he was angry. I could see that sitting him down made the situation less threatening and his volume decreased, not to arouse the clients in the home (the information on the clients is kept confidential). I asked him several open-ended questions about himself. At this time, the night manager saw the situation and pushed the emergency button. I was aware from her nonverbal messages that the police were on the way. Those 10 minutes felt like an eternity. However, the man opened up to me about his job loss and trying to keep up with insurance for one of his sick children. By the time the police arrived, the situation was de-escalated and the police also sat and talked with him for an hour. Finally, the man left peacefully.

I also learned that perception has a role in communication. I have seen that in my experiences. When I worked in the shelter, I had to see the perspective of the victims. It takes many times before a woman makes a decision to leave a violent relationship. Even though I had an opinion, I tried to understand the situation and listen empathically and repeat back (paraphrase) her feelings and anxieties.

Identity and culture impact communication. I noticed the reaction even in my day care to a child who wore braces on his legs. Sometimes his peers would not let them fit into their play, many times, he sat alone. It took months even after his braces were removed for the boy to mature socially and I encouraged him every day to take more risks. Dealing with stressed out parents was sometimes more difficult than taking care of the children. Once, there was a parent who was angry with me when her child made tortillas in my home because she thought my day care should have more educational activities. I found out later that she had difficulty with her cultural identity. Later, we became friends. I was glad that I was able to understand her perspective and move forward with our relationship. She also began to trust me and open up to me about her life.

Marriage is the most intimate of the one-on-one relationships. I've seen how raising children can become a priority and the relationship takes a back seat. My husband and I have taken our first vacation together ever after 20 years of marriage. I learned that you have to make relationships a priority or they can start to get stagnant. The priest at our parish recommended that we take time each week just to listen and get to know each other. This has helped us face changes in the empty nest phase of our lives.

Assertiveness is another skill I've used in conflict situations. If I don't say what's on my mind, I often act passively angry. Several of us read the book *Getting to Yes* by Fisher and Ury (1991) for an in-service training, which helped me see that there is often a win-win solution, but it takes both parties to share their needs. Often, we wind up with Lose-Lose or Lose-Win because we hide our interests and just stick to our position. In addition, I was able to attend training on mediation for children and adults given by the Mediation Project. During the mediation training, we were given a scenario and I had to play the neutral party to mediate and work through the steps of resolution. The first step was to let the parties vent. Then, they could work through the solution process. In many schools, children are trained to be mediators for conflicts. It was amazing to watch a video of elementary school children who were trained as mediators.

At Head Start, I realized that when talking to a two-year-old, I need to bend down, get at their level, and speak at their level. I learned how babies need touch in order to thrive. Nonverbal and verbal messages interrelate—support, add, help, and emphasize ideas. We use nonverbal messages to help the child with literacy by pronouncing words with emphasis, using exaggerated facial expressions and even music and dance. It's amazing to watch how their communication skills improve with their social and intellectual development.

Communication is a complex process where the need to adapt to the situation is very important. It sometimes is interrupted by noise, which can be as simple as a noisy classroom or as complex as the thoughts in our heads. This is also referred to as intrapersonal communication or communication with yourself. I noticed that even giving myself positive messages impacts the way I related to others. Interpersonal skills are ones that I can constantly learn and improve upon.

Supporting Documentation
Document 1—Letter from supervisor
Document 2—Certificate of training—Mediation project
Document 7—Annotated bibliography
Document 8—Performance evaluation

Small Group Communication
At Head Start we work with the children in groups. Even in the five-year-old groups, leaders emerge and the children take on different roles. We use a child-centered approach and we integrate children with debilities in our groups with children who do not have disabilities. Our group work is designed to enhance the cognitive and social development of the children and their families. As a group leader, I have to be sensitive to time and task (we have 130 children in our school and share resources and classrooms). I also have to be aware of group dynamics; such as, where two children sit next to each other may impact their concentration. I notice that the kids knew when I wasn't listening or was just faking it, and they acted out. It takes hard work and concentration to be attentive to the group.

Also, I worked with groups of adults at the shelter (I was not the therapist but the assistant). Just from observing great communicators such as the group therapist, I was able to make adjustments in my skills. I noticed how they used group rules or norms, for instance, that a person did not have to talk. Then, the group leader reminded the group of the rule that they had agreed upon (See Document 6). When I contributed, I tried never to interrupt, but I noticed sometimes there was usually a dominate person. When that occurred, we tried to make comments such as "let's hear from someone else." I've observed that turn-taking could be difficult for both children and adults. I also became aware of the role of the summarizer. Sometimes, this role was very important to bring across the points already covered.

In the Head Start work place I could observe different types of leadership styles. Some of the bosses were more rigid (authoritarian) about how things were run and the decisions to set schedules and policies. Others used a more democratic style and heard everyone's voice on problems and scheduling. Even though this style took more work, I saw the results were better. I saw that the laissez faire leadership style in one teacher who sort of let the group do what they wanted. This person did not last long in our team environment. Also, we were able to attend a conference in literacy and I heard talks from visionary leaders in the Latino community who were setting the direction for the future of education. I was able to witness leadership styles that motivated me to continue my education.

Supporting Documentation
Document 1—Letter from supervisor
Document 5 —Conference brochure—"Vision for the Future of Biliteracy Instruction"
Document 6—Group rules
Document 7—Annotated bibliography
Document 8—Performance evaluation
Document 9—Transcript

Conclusion

A supportive, open climate and adaptability are important in communication. Effective communication takes time, effort, and concentration to overcome the barriers. My communication skills have improved because I use them on a daily basis and have observed other mentors with excellent classroom management and facilitation skills. I hope to use and improve upon my skills in the classroom, at home, and with my co-workers by listening to the feedback from my supervisors and obtaining even more training in my profession.

APPENDIX 7

Sample Three-Part Competencies

Depending on the college's requirements, Maria could use a three-part format to describe her learning. See sample below:

DESCRIPTION OF EXPERIENCE	LEARNING FROM EXPERIENCE	DOCUMENTATION
	Topic 1: Public Speaking	
Prepared and presented 20 presentations on domestic violence and prevention to children, teens, and parents for La Familia during a two-and-a-half-year time period.	Adapted effectively to the age and experience of the audience.	1—Letters from supervisors
	Organized a presentation into an introduction, body, and conclusion.	3—Statistics on presentations
	Prepared appropriate handouts and visual aids for the audiences that were attractive, accurate, and free of errors.	7—Annotated bibliography
	Paid careful attention to delivery aspects such as eye contact, volume, pauses, facial expressions, tone, rate, and body language.	8—Performance evaluations
	Prepared and rehearsed so that the transitions between points sounded natural.	
	Managed nervousness to appear confident and composed.	
	Eliminated filler words such as "um" by pausing silently.	

(continued)

Description of Experience	Learning from Experience	Documentation
Prepared and delivered a formal PowerPoint presentation to a grant committee (La Familia).	Read the requirements and organized the speech to meet the requirements. Paid careful attention to purpose (information and persuasion) and needs of audience (result-oriented, time-stressed, and focused). Used PowerPoint effectively by not filling the slides with too much written text and building one idea per slide. Found current and reliable sources for statistics to persuade the audience of the need to re-fund the project. Timed the speech to meet the limits. Answered questions truthfully.	4—Speech and PowerPoint slides
Led three-, four- and five-year-old children for two years in lesson plans, music classes, and activities (Head Start).	Used classroom management techniques consistently. Used exaggerated gestures and nonverbal communication to maintain the children's interest. Spoke clearly to help children with literacy. Used an appropriate level vocabulary.	1—Letters from supervisors
Worked with a group on formal classroom presentations.	Designed visual aids and handouts to reflect all of the speaker's key ideas. Used a consistent format. Practiced presentation with the entire group to get feedback.	4—Speech and PowerPoint slides 9—Transcript

(continued)

DESCRIPTION OF EXPERIENCE	LEARNING FROM EXPERIENCE	DOCUMENTATION
Topic 2: Interpersonal Communication		
Worked with children at Head Start.	Understood, observed, and appreciated the Latino culture. Used nonverbal messages to interact with young children.	8—Performance evaluations
Worked in a domestic violence shelter two-and-a-half years doing intakes and educational outreach (La Familia).	Respected the confidentiality of all clients. Understood how a woman's desire to leave may be misperceived. Used de-escalation (sitting, talking quietly) with a conflict with an angry perpetrator until the police arrived. Read and applied *Getting to Yes* (Fisher and Ury, 1991). Attended and applied mediation training from the Mediation Project. Taught school children a step-by-step conflict resolution process. Appreciated the complexity of human communication.	2—Certificate of training—Intake skills
Managed a licensed day care in my home for seven years.	Worked effectively with parents to hear their concerns. Began a strong friendship with a parent from my day care when she disclosed the root of biases as a Latina woman. Learned to withhold first impressions and judgments in order to listen more effectively. Worked with a disabled boy to help him mature socially. Appreciated that touch could help a baby thrive.	9—Letter from day care mom

(continued)

DESCRIPTION OF EXPERIENCE	LEARNING FROM EXPERIENCE	DOCUMENTATION
Married for 20 years. Raised (with my husband) two sons.	Learned to take more time for dates with my husband. Taught my sons respect for all races and for women.	
Topic 3: Small Group Communication		
Led small groups in Head Start classrooms and interacted with staff.	Learned a child-centered approach and methods to integrate children with disabilities.	5—Conference brochure
	Observed different leadership styles (authoritarian, laissez-faire) and how the democratic supervisors allowed everyone's concerns to be heard.	8—Performance evaluations
	Practiced asking and answering questions without defensiveness.	
	Attended a conference and witnessed visionary leadership.	
	Appreciated how a leader could affect the climate of the whole organization.	
Led discussions with groups of teens. Assisted therapists in groups at La Familia.	Divided the teen girls from the boys during the discussion period in order to get better responses.	8—Performance evaluations
	Learned and applied group rules.	
	Learned to handle monopolizers.	
	Appreciated the role of a facilitator to help bring members to a new awareness.	6—Group rules
	Observed and practiced the role of summarizer.	

APPENDIX 8

Sample Letter of Verification

[Identities and company names are fictional.]

(Letterhead used)

Dear Portfolio Evaluator,

This letter testifies that Maria Rodriquez was employed at La Familia on a part-time basis during the period of Nov. 2000 to May 2002. I was the coordinator of the grant program and the domestic violence shelter and hired Maria. Maria worked in our shelter and assisted with an educational grant-funded domestic violence prevention programs in the office, in schools, and in the community.

During her employment, Maria used strong communication skills in numerous settings. She interacted effectively with our clients on the telephone, in person, and in classrooms. Maria used mature judgment in respecting the confidentiality of our clients and listening to their needs in order to accurately reflect the client's situation on our intake forms. I think one of her strengths was her ability to ask questions and to listen empathically to the answers. Many of our clients came in crisis situations and Maria helped them make the transition. Maria was called on numerous times to provide translation for our Spanish-speaking clients. She adapted well to stressful situations. Maria gave a presentation to our grant committee, which was well received. Maria also learned to overcome her shyness in public speaking by providing training in the classroom to children and parents. She was able to adapt her language and visual aids to both groups effectively. Maria's dedication to raising her children gave her the ability to relate well to other parents and children at the shelter. On her performance evaluation, Maria's communication skills were ranked high (4.5 out of possible 5).

I wish Maria all the best in her educational endeavors. Please feel free to contact me for more information.

Sincerely,

[Name of supervisor, title, address, e-mail address, phone number]

A P P E N D I X 9

Sample Faculty Evaluation

Methods of submission and assessment vary from college to college. For instance:

- Is the portfolio submitted as one petition for all subject areas or separate submissions for each subject area?
- Do individual faculty members evaluate the portfolio or is there a panel of evaluators (who are subject matter experts)?
- Are there specific criteria for credit based on outcomes or general criteria based on college level learning or competencies?
- Is the portfolio given a grade of credit/no credit (most common) or a letter grade?

Excerpt from faculty evaluation of Maria's portfolio:

Generally, the committee found that Maria's portfolio was well organized and well documented. The learning chronology set the context for her learning. The writing was at college level but had several grammatical errors. The petitioner requested credits that are aligned with her goal of associate degree in early childhood education. The committee assigns credit for learning that is the equivalent of a 70% or C minus level or higher.

The competencies for First Aid and Piano Class I were strong and complete, and the supporting documentation was sufficient for the awards. The only learning gap identified in the first aid petition was the recognition for continuing education as the first aid and CPR standards are updated. The student showed above the competency levels for introductory learning in music theory and applications for special needs children. The inclusion of dance and song techniques used by the petitioner impressed the panel. The methods petition showed experience in the classroom and understanding of literacy but lacked a broader understanding of education principles. Maria will benefit from her coursework in educational theorists and principles of multiculturalism. The petition for Comparing Cultures demonstrated mature awareness, but was awarded two credits due to the minimal experiential learning of cultures outside the Latino culture. The demonstration of learning in Introduction to Communication was enhanced by the other petitions including the discussion of culture and educational methods. The documentation, especially the text of the speech Maria presented before the grant committee, demonstrated above-average speech-preparation skills. The petitioner's experience was adequately verified with letters from two supervisors.

See notes in the portfolio from faculty subject matter experts on the rationale for the assessment.

The faculty assessing committee awards the following:

Petition for 14 credits (based on quarter hours.) Awarded 11 credits in the following areas *[no grades assigned because this college's awards are credit/no credit]*

Early Childhood Education Methods (2)—Average rating

Comparing Cultures (2)—Average rating

Introduction to Communication (3)—Average rating with above average in public speaking

First Aid (1)—Above average rating

Piano Class I (3)—Above average rating

A copy of this record will be sent to the records office for transcription.

The student has 30 days to appeal this decision to the chair of the assessment committee. Appeals policies are located at the assessment office.

Glossary of Terms

AACRAO—The American Association of Collegiate Registrars and Admissions Officers (www.aacrao.org)

academic year—The time period of academic instruction, which is divided into semesters, quarters, or trimesters.

accreditation—Recognition of a college by an independent private organization. Accreditation is a factor in the transfer of credits from institution to institution.

accreditation mill—An entity that unethically awards accreditations to colleges that do not meet widely accepted standards.

accredited institution—Colleges and universities that have acquired accreditation of their programs.

ACE—Adult Council on Education (www.acenet.edu)

ACT—American College Testing program, which administrates aptitude and achievement tests.

admissions—The application process completed by a student in order to enter a college. Admissions tasks may include completing an application, requesting transcripts, or taking competency exams.

adult-friendly colleges—A term that describes colleges that provide services for the adult learner.

adult learner—A student who is over the age of 25, financially independent, and working, as distinguished from the traditional-student (typically an 18-to-24-year-old who entered college immediately after high school).

advisor—A person employed by the college (often a faculty member) who assists students with degree plan requirements, transcription of previous credit, and prior learning assessment options.

articulation—The system used by colleges to compare courses and specify equivalencies.

articulation agreement—Agreements among colleges or programs regarding the transfer of credit. For example, a four-year college may have an articulation agreement with a two-year college to seamlessly transfer a student's credit.

artifacts—Also known as "documentation" or "exhibits," these are items that demonstrate or verify a student's learning.

assessment—The measurement of learning based on criteria and indicators. When referring to prior learning assessment, the process of defining, documenting, measuring and evaluating a student's non-college or experientially-gained knowledge, skills, and competencies for the purpose of awarding college-level credit.

assessment fee—The costs of assessment of a student's learning for college-level credit. Fees vary from institution to institution and may be one lump sum or changed per credit.

assessor—An individual with appropriate knowledge and skill who is responsible for measuring a person's learning. Also known as a faculty evaluator, this is a faculty member or expert in the subject area being assessed, who is responsible for evaluating a candidate's prior learning.

associate degree—A degree awarded to a student after completing the equivalent of two years of full-time coursework (typically 60–64 semester hours or 105–120 quarter hours in the U.S.).

bachelor's degree—A degree awarded to a student after completing the equivalent of four years of full-time coursework (typically 120–128 semester hours in the U.S.). In other countries the bachelor's degree generally takes three years.

Bloom's Taxonomy—Benjamin Bloom described three domains of educational activities: cognitive, affective, and psychomotor (knowledge, attitude, and skills).

CAEL—The Council for Adult and Experiential Learning (www.cael.org) is a national nonprofit organization that creates and manages effective learning strategies for working adults through partnerships with employers, higher education, government, and labor. CAEL publishes the standards for the assessment of learning that colleges use to create policies and procedures for their prior learning assessment programs.

case study—A tool the assessor can use that allows a learner to demonstrate his or her learning as it applies to a specific situation.

certificate—A document verifying participation by a person in a training or other organized learning experience. Certificates may represent levels of that participation ranging from only attendance to attendance with assessment of the desired learning outcomes.

CEU—Typically given in training courses, a *continuing education unit* is often awarded for educational experiences that help meet the designation of a professional organization such as a teacher or a lab technician. CEUs alone are rarely considered the equivalent of academic credit.

challenge exam—An examination written by instructors at their respective colleges that is given to learners to assess whether their learning equates to a college course. The challenge exam may be similar in content to the final exam given in a course.

CHEA—The Council on Higher Education Accreditation

CLEP—The College-Level Examination Program, a national program that provides standardized examinations in a number of subject matters allowing students to earn college credit for their learning (www.collegeboard.com).

college—In the U.S., an institution offering programs leading to the associate (two-year) degree, bachelor's (four-year) degree, or a higher degree. Or, a specific college in a university may refer to a part of an institution or field within the university (e.g., Daniels Business College at the University of Denver).

College Board—Publishers of CLEP exams (www.collegeboard.com).

college level—A determination made by faculty, colleges, and accrediting bodies. Course competencies, course descriptions, and course syllabi assist in recognizing the type, depth, and breadth of learning that is considered college level.

community college—A school offering programs leading to the associate degree. May offer non-credit courses and labs on such topics as writing, English as a second language, or math. Sometimes referred to as a junior college.

competence—A demonstrable capability based on an underlying knowledge basis within a specified context.

competence-based credit model—The assignment of credit to demonstrated and assessed competence rather than to a specific body of knowledge or subject matter.

contexts—Circumstances surrounding a place or time. In prior learning assessment, one measure of a candidate's learning is whether the learning is applicable or transferable to other contexts.

continuing education—Courses offered in a number of venues, such as schools or community education centers, that are targeted to adults. In some cases, the courses may be offered for college credit.

course—A specific unit of instruction, such as a course in microeconomics or abnormal psychology.

course challenge—A request for credit based on the demonstration of knowledge, specified learning outcomes, and/or competence equivalent to an existing course in a curriculum.

credit—A unit used to record and measure a formal course, typically based on the number of hours spent in class each week.

critical incidents—Events that resulted in changed thinking, attitudes, or actions.

curriculum—A prescribed set of courses for an area of specialization (e.g., engineering, biology, computer science).

degree—College degrees are earned by completing a specified number of courses or other studies in accordance with a program design acceptable to the college or university and subject to their requirements. Some common degrees are the associate degree and bachelor's degree.

degree plan—A detailed description of the program and courses an applicant or enrolled student plans to pursue. The process of mapping out coursework to complete a degree is also known as academic, degree, or coursework planning.

DETC—Distance Education and Training Council, a type of accreditation given to colleges that differs from regional accreditation.

diploma—The certificate that shows that a certain type of study has been completed. In some cases diplomas are awarded for completing a degree or course of study.

diploma mill—An unethical, unaccredited institution that issues a worthless degree for a fee.

discipline—A broad field of study, such as history, psychology, or computer science (as opposed to "subject," which is more specialized, such as "history of the post-reconstruction period" or "adolescent psychology").

distance learning—Also known as online, distance education, or distributed learning, this type of learning relies on educational technologies such as the Internet, CDs, or video for delivery.

documentation—Evidence that supports the claim for credit for prior learning experience. Documents, artifacts, or other forms of products that represent what a person knows or can do (i.e., has learned) and that are used to substantiate an individual's claim for credit in an assessment process. Evidence may be direct (what the person says or represents regarding his/her learning) or indirect (what others say about the learning). Documentation may be in the form of transcripts, professional licenses or certificates, records of apprenticeship, certificates of completion of company training, official job descriptions, letters, news clippings, products produced by the student such as books, paintings, computer programs, etc.

DSST (DANTES Subject Standard Tests)—Program administers equivalency exams for military and civilians (see http://www.getcollegecredit.com/).

electives—Also known as general electives, open electives, or free electives, these are courses taken to fulfill degree requirements that are not requirements for the major or core studies, but selected to fill a degree program.

electronic portfolio—Portfolio that is hosted on the Web with programs that interface with a database, allowing portfolio contents to be uploaded and viewed online. Also known as e-portfolio, Webfolio, or digital portfolio, they are commonly used to build career portfolios, demonstrate writing, or show competencies in teacher education programs.

evaluator—Also known as a faculty assessor, person who is responsible for evaluating a candidate's prior learning.

experiential learning—Any learning in which the learner is in direct touch with the realities being studied. This learning may be sponsored (as in work/study arrangements, internships, apprenticeships) or it may be acquired informally through hands-on experience and practice through work, travel, personal development, or community service. It is learning that has been gained as a result of reflecting upon the events or experiences in one's life in contrast to formal education.

faculty—Those who are responsible for teaching in colleges and universities. The common titles given to faculty, in ascending order, are: lecturer, instructor, assistant professor, associate professor, professor. In addition, schools may employ teaching assistants who are graduate students and part-time or adjunct faculty who have expertise in a specific area. A few colleges call their faculty "mentors" or "learning facilitators" regardless of their rank.

fees—Money paid to a school for purposes other than tuition. Fees for assessment services are paid upfront.

financial aid—A term that includes scholarships, loans, fellowships, tuition reductions, or other methods of financial payment to the college. Many schools have a financial aid department to manage financial aid questions.

full-time student—Normally considered a student who is enrolled in 12 semester hours or more of credit in a given term.

GED tests—General Education Development tests measure a student's knowledge and academic skills. The GED is considered the equivalent of a traditional high school degree.

goals statement—One of the components of a portfolio or other evidence presented for assessment toward credit. The intent of a goals statement is to help a person in the PLA process clarify his or her short and long term personal, professional and/or educational goals to set a context for the assessment process.

grade-point average—The average score a student has made in all of his or her classes, weighted by the number of credits or units for each class. Also called G.P.A.

graduate—A person who has earned a degree from a school. In the U.S. graduate programs are offered beyond the bachelor's (also known as postgraduate) degree.

Kolb's model of experiential learning—David Kolb's four-stage cycle of learning from experience illustrates how experiential learning is a cycle involving concrete experience, reflection observation, abstract conceptualization, and active experimentation.

learning autobiography—A narrative that gives an account of a person's lifelong learning.

letter of validation—A letter written by an outside party used to verify a student's learning.

major—The subject or discipline in which a student specializes. Using it as a noun, one can have a major in math, sociology, business studies, etc. As a verb, one can major in these subjects. Each school has regulations that determine how many courses must be completed in one's major subject to fulfill the requirements of the degree.

mind map—Also known as concept map, a technique that a writer uses to create a preliminary visual outline of the concepts or ideas.

minor—The secondary subject or academic department outside the major in which a student takes concentrated coursework (generally, four or more courses in an area of study).

multiple intelligences—Categories that describe people's preferred learning styles, behavioral and working styles, and natural strengths. In addition to the basic seven intelligences (logical-mathematical, linguistic, spatial, musical, body-kinesthetic, interpersonal, and intrapersonal), Howard Garner has added naturalist, spiritual/existential, and moral.

narrative—An essay with personal reflections, anecdotes, and insights.

OWL—Online Writing Lab—A type of writing lab with resources and help offered to students that is accessible from the Web.

part-time student—Normally, a student who is enrolled in less than 12 hours of credit per term.

portfolio—A collection of evidence in support of a person's claim for credit through a prior learning assessment process. A formal communication presented by the student to the college as part of a petition requesting credit or recognition for learning outside the college classroom. The portfolio must make its case by identifying learning clearly and succinctly, and it must provide sufficient supporting information and documentation so that faculty can use it, alone or in combination with other evidence, as the basis for their evaluations (Lamdin, 1992, p. 84). The portfolio is the package used in assigning academic credit for learning.

pre-requisites—Courses that must be completed first before enrolling in more advanced coursework.

pre-writing—Exercises used to assist writers to warm-up (gather ideas and organize thoughts) before writing.

prior learning assessment (PLA)—A term used by colleges and universities to describe the process of earning college credit certification or advanced standing, from learning acquired through a student's work, training, volunteer experiences, and personal life. Also known as assessment of prior learning (APL), prior learning assessment and recognition (PLAR), and flexible assessment (a term used in the U.K.).

proprietary information—Company material that is considered confidential.

registrar—The college official responsible for keeping records on the enrollment and academic standing of students. The registrar also must attest to the validity of transcripts submitted for admission to advance standing.

resumé—Although usually defined as a summary of one's work experience, for purposes of assessment, the resumé includes all experiences that may have resulted in learning: date, sources, the nature of the work (or hobby or independent learning of any kind), and the learnings acquired.

semester hour—An amount of credit earned in a course, normally representing one classroom hour per week for a semester.

signature of authenticity—A signed statement that the contents of the portfolio are true and accurate representations.

supporting documentation—See "documentation."

syllabus—A detailed outline of a course written by a faculty member that may include course goals, textbooks, instructor contact information, learning outcomes, schedules, policies course topics, evaluation, and grading criteria.

tacit knowledge—An untapped source of knowledge used by learners who are largely unaware of its richness.

TOEFL—The Test of English as a Foreign Language (www.ets.org/toefl/), which measures English language proficiency.

transcript—An official document that lists courses taken by a student, grades received, and credit awarded (degree awarded). Official transcripts have the imprint of the school's seal. Unofficial transcripts are copies without the official seal.

transfer student—A student who has earned credit in one school, and then applies the credit to another school's program.

transitional phrases—Words and phrases used by writers to help the reader follow the chronology of events.

tuition—The amount a college charges for courses (U.S. term only).

undergraduate—Period of study leading up to the awarding of the bachelor's degree.

university—An educational institution that usually comprises one or more colleges. Many universities offer adult-oriented or adult-friendly programs.

Index